Social Networking Objectives For The New Millenium And Beyond

SOCIAL NETWORKING OBJECTIVES FOR THE NEW MILLENIUM AND BEYOND

HOW TO MICROMANAGE A ETHICAL PROFESSIONAL SOCIALIZED WHOLISTIC SOCIAL NETWORKING AND ENTERTAINMENT CAFÉ IN ANY TYPE OF CULINAIRY SERVICES OUTLET OR DRIVE-THRU WITH A RESTAURANTE OR CUSTOMER SERVICES AREA

A GUIDE TO DEVELOPING PROSPERITY PARTNERSHIP

This book is about how to legislate
green catering policy guide lines
for the new millennium
and beyond

VERA MOON

To order additional copies of this book, contact:
Xlibris Corporation
1-888-795-4274
www.Xlibris.com
Orders@Xlibris.com
107638

⊥ Every business needs a valuable social networking forum or site customers need to be able to share social reviews with each other.

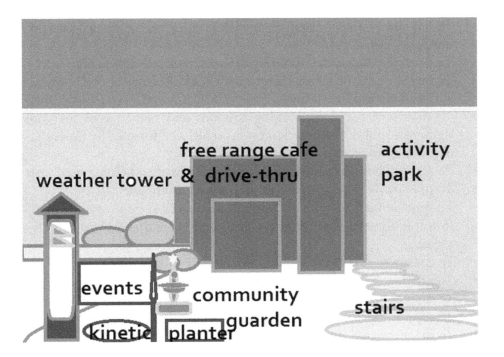

⊥ WHY DO WE NEED A SOCIALIZED FOOD SERVICES INDUSTRY?

- To unite persons with the same educational goals and travel plans
- To provide a lawful gathering place where freedom of assembly is guaranteed
- To provide a venue to citizens where they can learn how to use social networking medias to share games, discuss news events, etc.
- To provide a venue to persons where the custom of grace is respected as a certified treaty
- To provide a network of professionals to customers that delivers customized services
- To provide a venue to clients that wish to enjoy peaceful social activities during sunset
- To provide a venue that disseminates new product demonstrations
- To provide a venue where citizens may hold discourse on web business and midway media culture
- To distribute social networking coupons and event passes for book signings at public information events scheduled for specific times each day, and so forth.
- To network business addenda so all staff will have their housing needs met
- To provide the staff with a holistic work environment
- To provide buffets twice daily—public speaker at noon, public open-forum testimony after brunch—so all may share dreams and concerns together
- To use art to support fellowship discussions and services
- To provide media networking to the public
- To support public campaigns to promote customized recycling services
- To support harvest, Passover, and new moon festivals
- To magnify toasts for open discourse
- To network friendship-circle events
- To celebrate unification at winter fest midway-venues
- To promote green card networking
- To provide stewardship to singles searching for professional development partnerships or prosperity partnership services
- To provide a certified social networking forum for singles searching for love, romance, custom service, and professional partnership
- To archive seasonal customer services reporting

you have your niech place in the global food chain

believe it!

1

Reflections on the history of industrial marketing and retailed monopoly ploys and how a map of unity should be considered at any time

It was a beautiful day, and the rain had stopped. The fountains were music that quelled the pain of any anger during the skate club trial events. It was so nice to walk near the condos where the fast-food drive-through staff was in evening. In my dream of the new city zone just constructed, they had everything they needed for comfort within walking distance.

No one was ever alone, broke, or friendless, wandering like a lost star with a worn-down soul with only tragedy to face as the gray clouds whisk past in the wind, illuminating nothing. Even at work, everything was so perfect, organized. Every detail measured to suit a perfect design template that was a charismatic interactive, living puzzle. In many places, corporations were being bought by recycling firms, and some were still trying to finance plans to restore drainage systems, but not anywhere in these trademark condo complexes.

Everything was perfectly fit and rhythmically manicured as the staff had a full-service spa and salon only for them; it was so special. The staff was cared for so well. They knew they were in good shape for the customers that needed them. They were well prepared as their illustrated application form had also tests to keep them informed of schedule specifics to expect.

After the interview and hiring process were complete, the team had visits from their recycling firm reps, entertainers, craft guilds, toy designers, motivational speakers, system designers, maintenance workshop hosts, and customer-relations training teams. Any educational CDs could be bought or taken from the library. It was a very effective and efficient team with all the process requirements for training, team building, and managing effective new design workshops and bonus extras.

At least once a year, home party specialists would cater to their every whim! They made annual contracts from birth sign energy totems. Real music of the soul. Dancing before work got them cooking and ready for active duty.

At every new moon by zodiac seal, each tenant got an ad mail census review to make certain they had no financial hardships or other socioeconomic hardships.

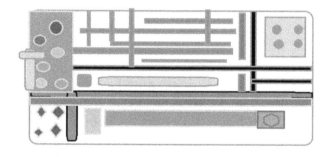

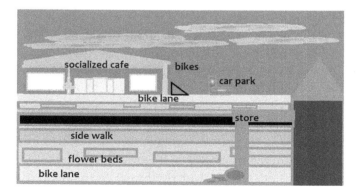

We are earth, wind, soul, light, music, from, water. Consider that some people are very gifted. They can weave maps to heal broken hearts.

Whenever a plant is pruned or plucked at harvest, it is a time to observe how to mend any rends. Plants are sculpted as the wind and rain and sun multiply. These elements nourish development. Plants are food, music, progressive inspiration that will energize all activity. When we eat, we are broken like an offering at communion time so we are sensitive to the needs of others who require our custom bondable services.

That whole cycle of nourishment is an ecoculture trend, thus our meals need to be custom ordered to suit all spiritual and metaphysical needs we have. As daybreak awakens the dew, we are broken in spirit so we are ready to stand and prepare to witness our service vows at harvest.

The sunrise is a blessing on all in the midst of the shadows of the earth and the elements of the seasons. A meal is a form of inspirational, interactive poetry we partake in to prepare our soul to make ready each heart for rendering service.

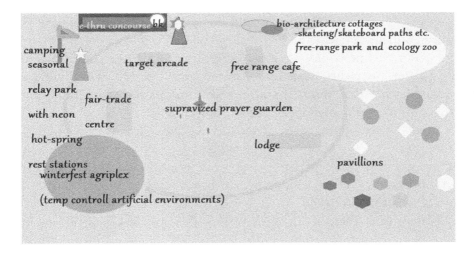

It was really nice to be in a café garden with birth sign energy totems that surrounded you. You paid for service with tokens that were embossed with an agenda seal. You believed you would be taken care of there, and you believed you could get all the service and community information you needed. You knew you were at a booth where you would meet people that had the same common interests as you did. You knew because you could make your social networking plans from the booth with the menu to plan your business day including personal support.

There were events planned for any activity you could imagine. If you were into sports, it was not just a fad to number crowds and place bets.

It was a charismatic social science. The sport videos taught you how to exercise and share burdens with others in need. You learned how to be a part of unconditional-acts-of-kindness campaigns that would end strife and conflict. Fair-trade peppers were hot! Free-range farm barbecue music was a real vision of how to build a nest to enjoy real peace and security year round with all the fixings.

It was a nice place for dinner after a walk in the park or a session at the wind chimes gallery—a community center with a gym and transcendental meditation arts school. Entertainments began at four A.M. Barbecue sauce for apple pie was always fresh and full of good spirit, cooked to the mulled-over beat of modern electronica. The ovens and barbecues really cooked by the pulse of the musical sunset color symbols as a plan was weaved to bond all souls to one true, pure vision of unification, and all hearts could be warmed as tears of dew were dried and bottled to kindle the flame for peace twenty-four hours.

If you were an art fan, you could make a project toast any time you wished You submitted a yellow docket. The club was open twenty-four hours, and anyone could make project proposals, or you could toast the color poems that surrounded you as the music played. The digital art changed with the rhythms. If you just liked to talk lots, you could join a public forum on the digital café menu.

This was a real modern social networking café that anyone could use to earn a profit. Even if they were only there to play a game, even that could become a charismatic experience! The business motto was "Peace is sharing and cooperation." When you were there, it was like you were all aboard the train of a lifetime in 3-D!

If they were there to find friendship, that too was available on the menu or by customized request. Fair-trade rally news and promotions in small towns like Melville or any other anywhere on earth could eliminate poverty, crime, aloneness, and decadence as winter-carnival media networks expanded from one town to the next after inter-racial unity conferrences with free transportations, peace-walk caroling and candle-lighting and faith-healing seminars were promoted.

It was, to some, better than the Burger King party cruise line or cruisers line for vintage auto memorabilia fans (a really nice place to enjoy spicy onion, sweet and sour sauce condiments.

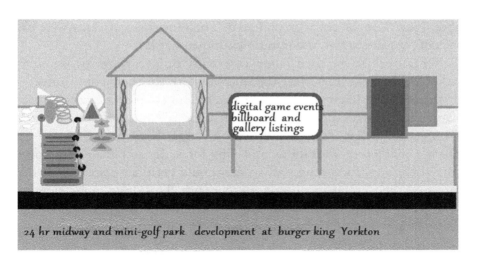

24 hr midway and mini-golf park development at burger king Yorkton

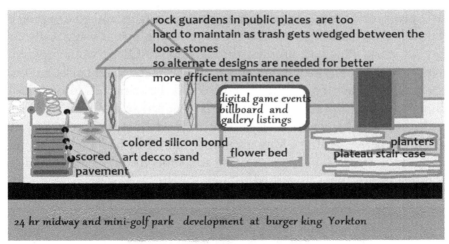

24 hr midway and mini-golf park development at burger king Yorkton

Many restaurants now had a membership; regular customers had a card to show that by treaty they were a preferred customer. Customers that scheduled a party at the venue or a meeting could also customize transportations available to guests, a limo from any historical* epoch or for any specific occasion, and the color could be customized. Customers could select a card with the embossed logo of any issue they supported and could donate a portion of sales proceeds to that cause every time they used their logo or holiday theme card.

They would receive membership news and events catalogue mailing from the group they joined. They could add on game faction logos, other logos, icon flags, or crests as preferred. The same type of cards were also available at game stores and fashion boutiques at plazas.

Where people began to buy cars with Burger King logos on the dashboard because they liked the midway park space that surrounded it or because they liked the Burger King biz lunch and the personalized, customized service apps downloads on their cell phones from the king of burger land web. The drive-in with a Burger King plaza and deli had Internet marketing workshops and labs for staff, and many employees work study apps for young staff so they could get their grades up as they improved their professional service experience. This drive-in location had a Burger King logo and biofuel flags. And most of the customers had a customer service passport so they could get coupon deals at any Burger King-sponsored event.

It was a cool place to work, hang out, play games, shop, and make travel plans for holidays. It was nice to pick up burgers and go camping on weekends after work. There was no stress, no hang-ups. It was a really cool place to work. Plus you profited through their ROI network programs. Neon swifter brooms had: lights, side scrubbers, deodorizer packs, minivan attachments. The fryers and hoods could be cleaned automatically. Minibots picked up anything customers dropped in the park lot. Work was fun there. The place was a small miracle where midway events could be enjoyed before or after a king meal deal. The lobby had a small play area for children with waiting room seating and supervision. There were many sponsorship programs advertised.

drive-in playland, games park with: carding concourse

Available Services

1. Supervised children's play area with photographer/videographer available
2. Maps and official land treaty passports and a travel-planning service office on sites
3. Shopping concourse
4. Twenty-four-hour café and arcade
5. Social networking seminars (automated) and conference rooms ROI benefits
6. Community and tourism club info kits and event calendars
7. Public social events listings and participaction logo agendas
8. Camping gear and passes
9. Wildlife club brochures and membership kits
10. Tourism club media kits
11. Go Green biofuel station

The restrooms had taps that shut off automatically, and they were color temp correct. An occupied sign lit up automatically when anyone entered, and they were maintained by central vacuum stations for each lavatory. All the upgrades were part of the new millennium and beyond business building models or ecoculture modeling building societies would sponsor.

Everything was stainless and really easy to clean. All trash was vacuumed and deposited into a compacting bin. The cubes were sold to recycling firms.

Everything operated from a computerized timer. All the extra grease that was not evaporated from the angled drip trays was vacuum packaged and recycled. There was no waste, no landfill problem, no crevices to collect dust, grime, or dripping grease, and no waste could be caught in dangling cords under counters. Everything was in its place or refillable tube that could be refilled and measured like clockwork, as all had a time, place, and purpose. The drive-in plaza Burger King had the same meal deals and professional networking games for young children as all other locations did. There were games for children that taught them how to be a part of the team, how to get involved/evolved in custom game development workshops. All the children got free members club prizes and stickers for activities they participated in and based on their behavior while in line and while in the café. They could play games from one table to the next as the floor tile was a games map, and they could hand out coupons to anyone they wanted to, anytime.

The grounds were well maintained with a play park and fluorescent drive-through port for freight loading.

All the stockroom shelves had product labels, as did the cooler and ripe room, and all staff got personalized coats and freezer masks. The place was really designed to be fun to work in.

Besides all that website membership, guaranteed no request for employment was ever rejected. The company procedures operations manager, Manuel, would not allow any firings for any reason. Only hirings, relocations, bridging, and reassignments were permitted as constitutional. It was the same at any other location as follows pictorially.

lazer target games if on target the logo lights up no weapons configurations only sight/reflex game by a yoga priest(baptist) that stops kung-fu crime in hollywood.

moving or stationary targets also farm-gate / trappers targets and wreath art games for nature train and river-

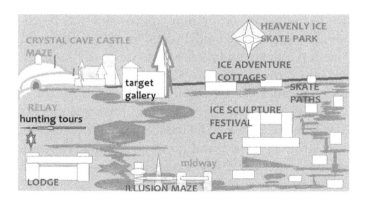

CRYSTAL CAVE CASTLE MAZE

HEAVENLY ICE SKATE PARK

ICE ADVENTURE COTTAGES

target gallery

SKATE PATHS

RELAY
hunting tours

ICE SCULPTURE FESTIVAL CAFE

midway

LODGE

ILLUSION MAZE

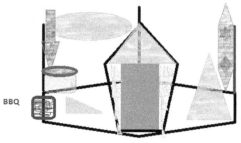

BBQ

this cute gazebo makes wind and rain and cloud patterns musical to entertain BBQ guests does creating this sound fun to you it is a beutiful place to enjoy ice cream and a movie on a rainy day agree?

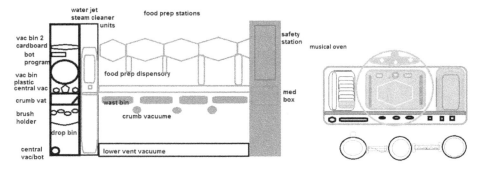

water jet
steam cleaner
units

food prep stations

safety station

musical oven

vac bin 2
cardboard
bot program

vac bin plastic
central vac

crumb vat

brush holder

drop bin

central vac/bot

food prep dispensory

wast bin

crumb vacuume

lower vent vacuume

med box

all food prep areas etc are cleaned by magnetic robots and
also each prep area ovens etc have cleaning stations right
beside them and fire safety units too

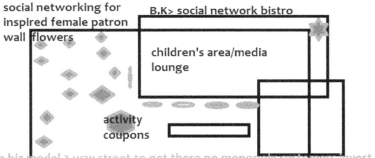

social networking for
inspired female patron
wall flowers

B.K> social network bistro

children's area/media
lounge

activity
coupons

a biz model 2 way street to get there no monopoly customers invest
personal time and money to secure a profit through shared
social networking contract interests.

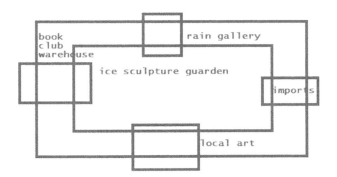

book
club
warehouse

rain gallery

ice sculpture guarden

imports

local art

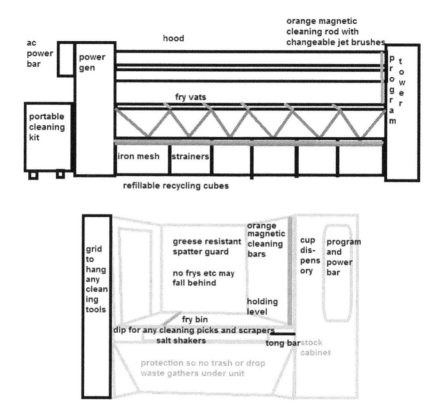

ac power bar | **power gen** | hood | orange magnetic cleaning rod with changeable jet brushes | **program tower**

fry vats

portable cleaning kit

iron mesh | **strainers**

refillable recycling cubes

grid to hang any cleaning tools

greese resistant spatter guard

no frys etc may fall behind

orange magnetic cleaning bars

cup dis-pens ory | program and power bar

holding level

fry bin

dip for any cleaning picks and scrapers

salt shakers

tong bar | stock cabinet

protection so no trash or drop waste gathers under unit

drip proof and stucco proof fry bin

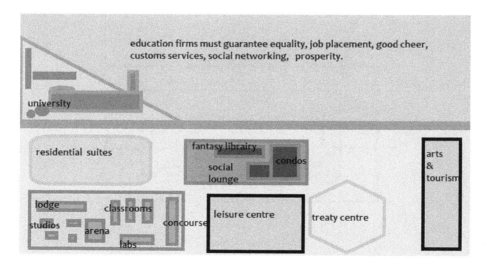

education firms must guarantee equality, job placement, good cheer, customs services, social networking, prosperity.

university

residential suites

fantasy library

social lounge

condos

arts & tourism

lodge

classrooms

studios

arena

concourse

leisure centre

treaty centre

labs

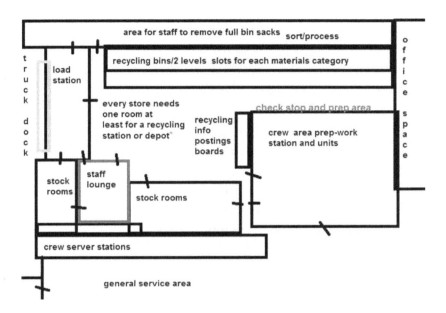

area for staff to remove full bin sacks   sort/process

office space

recycling bins/2 levels slots for each materials category

truck dock

load station

every store needs one room at least for a recycling station or depot"

recycling info postings boards

check stop and prep area

crew area prep-work station and units

stock rooms

staff lounge

stock rooms

crew server stations

general service area

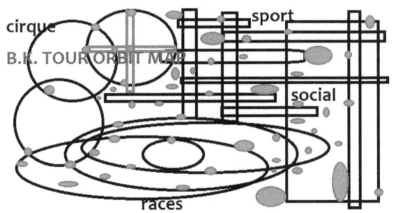

cirque

sport

B.K. TOUR ORBIT MAP

social

races

lazer target games   if on target the logo lights up no weapons configurations   only sight/reflex game   by a yoga priest(baptist) that stops kung-fu crime in hollywood.

moving or stationary targets

also farm-gate / trappers targets

and wreath art games for nature train and river-

They were all neat little venues, all the clubs that decided on the universal fair-trade policy to socialize their venue and train clients to invest. Workers were happy to be in uniform, ready for service. At the gourmet burger palace, the staff said they really felt like dancing on the sunny side of the street in their custom-tailored hats and professionally buffed shoes. The uniforms were custom fit at the salons. And there was a laying on of hands ceremony for every crew customer at fitting time, videotaped for their résumé or keepsakes albums. A song about the service employee was created there. Their employee card had a color-harmony karma code embossed in specific trade crest aura icons. It was all custom criterions for that genre of trusted service. All the crack patty hosts were celebrated at the first day of summer party with firecrackers for entertainment before custodial prayer services. The childlike were in crimson, and the ambitious were in their pattern copy demos with tie-dye emblems or press-on art. Some made their own costume. Everyone was a critic.

Some people would still ask though, Why should anyone want to socialize culinary service venues, theaters?

We need a reasonable food-service outlet that can guarantee customer satisfaction. The venue has a duty to serve all needs the customer has. This means that the staff dietitian nourishes the customer as the client portfolio prescribes. The customer needs to enjoy the meal, the company, the presentation, the environment, and the service should be balanced nutritionally and economically based on a personal schedule to suit the client as an individual. The preplanned activity of the customer must be charted and well nourished. This may be illustrated as any wordbook, Pictionary workbook, zodiac, or seasonal map or calendar. This may also be seen as a billboard, apartment, wall mosaic, or other agenda so all meals are lawfully and with benefit garnished. All venues should guarantee by law customer satisfaction, is palatable to digest. The experience of purposeful nourishment thus should be illustrated as a day-timer journal entry.

Theaters need to be socialized to make certain that all that share the same perspective are blessed as bond servants. Theater is a charismatic training system that should be used to unite bond servants.

There the prisoners rest together;
they hear not the voice of the oppressor.

—Job 3:18

What should we expect financially after visiting an imagined theater room at a digital art café?

Mutual investment profit.

2

Epicurian Rainbows

The city really shone bright after the rain that day. The sunrise song could lead anyone to heaven where friendship could be found. It was time to open the new Burger Palace. The digital billboard was lit in lightblue with rainbow highlights. This new café had a new teen menu just for teens. And there were also novelty items teens could take home. They really liked the place a lot, and opening day had a banner up saying We Salute Dominique. He was the teen that did all the electrical work to construct the burger palace. He was only fifteen years old.

Job 21:11

All the people that saluted him did not claim him as a king or submit to him as a dictator though. They just saluted him (Job 2-4) because he was the first teen to graduate on his birthday with a construction and maintenance contract. It would be his job to maintain and clean all the wiring done. It was a lifelong contract. The tools he used would make a video record of all the maintenance work that was concluded and would record the time used to complete the work. The burger palace was a dream come true. Teens constructed their primary place of business before graduation day.

The sword dances, once popular with the later clan, were not allowed on opening day, though all dance festival propaganda or any supreme dictatorship or autocracy with caste or class systems were not allowed. Dance and WWF moves were not promoted, as wrestling for tools was a form of unwanted torture and prejudicial subjugation that society was not in any need of.

The doorway had a digital abacus that was color-coded so that each customer group was recorded as their chip card was inserted in the doorway.

Their guest number was added on at the till with their table number for billing. There were about fifty there for the AM meal deal (an abbreviation for angry whopper meal deal). A toast with extra dipping sauce to all in agreement. No one should go to bed angry at their brother. There were about fifty there for breakfast, and the same group of fifty, as most had the ability, were usually there through drive-through before curfew hour began. There were no wrestling club gimmicks on Parents' Day nor T-shirts or key tag logos to divvy, though a few on board had Love Lives Here logos on keys and house party brochures to minister to persons at the bar and get them out of that situation of alcoholic delusion. They were mellow-yellow club supporters. Love Lives Here members had a group of new age barhoppers that picked people up at the bar then took them home to their abode for an new life ministry presentation on how to live an addiction-free lifestyle. They also had a meal deal special for the pick-me-up pep talk. Staff distributed Bike gift cards at the event. There were quite a few anti-native syndicate supporters there and also friendship-circle center members at the home party events.

Love Lives Here academics were all promoting good news calendars from their company room abound with coupon deals from Bike every Thursday and Friday night and other nights too as scheduled. They made a pledge of allegiance, as citizens and good neighbors and club supporters, to make certain all were well treated through a commercial sponsorship plan from the friendship center or other cultural or social organization.

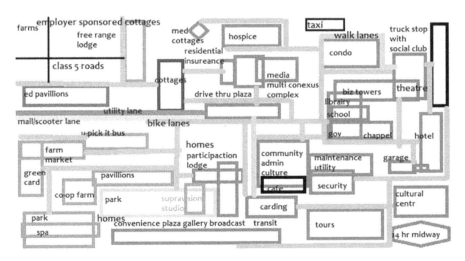

Everyone would accede to the programmer to gain extra points as good citizens. One man, a car salesman, suggested that people get credit like good drivers do if they did not take up drinking or smoking. So one of the home sales clubs for singles started to offer insurance deals to members, and they also signed up with the mellow-yellow Love Lives Here group. Singles club members got extra credit points on their citizenship card if they did not smoke or drink, and Smokers Anonymous club members got a free-meal-deal banquet and party at Burger King at the end of the year. They were easy to accommodate.

**Joes was the perfect manager. He was always polite, and if a new recruit did not have someone to have breakfast with at Burger King, he would soon surely find someone to be friend, mentor, lifelong business partner, or in-season fair-trade compact consultant or business development coach. He was a man that knew how to get organized from one to twenty-two, from *A* to *Z*. He was a quick thinker, knew a lot of adages, and was quick to add a trendy saying to any conversation. No man could accuse him of not being in vogue.

His conversations were never off tune, off-color, or offbeat. He was well studied and kept up-to-date on the most current cultural news events. He worked with seven media-promotions networking stewards. He catered to summer fair staff. His sons went and feasted in their houses, everyone in his day, and sent and called for their three sisters to eat and drink with them. Job 1:4. Their sisters were interior design consultants that made welcome wagon baskets with each new staff member that rented a condo or home after they became a Bike recruit. Job 1:6. They did not have a service customs calendar that was at all alike to the Burger Baron disco agenda or the other drive-me-wild style max menu drive-throughs with dress codes or wild game renaissance dessert menus. Games menu agendas were socialization media not adjit prop theater events.

Early in the morning, Art Carter turned on the electronic abacus before the first till opened. The fair-trade torch was lit at the gate to the hedge that was used to mark the paths to follow in the minigolf arena part of the midway fanfare there. Job 1:11. Anyone that entered could leave with a profit. It was not just a place to throw cash around, to waste time, or try to buy friendship or a popular nickname.

Job 1:16. Sunset musical games were tests to make certain none were oppressed, demised, or undermined. The games fair had games that were presented at the Valentine's Day banquet at the history museum. Job 1:10.

There were also remakes of Italian army games from regions where Nazis made agreements to abstain from war. Also, the ruins of the bunkers of brain XXX (job 9:28, 31) were recreated. He was an evil dictator that plotted oppression and extortion crimes by attacking free speech and free press laws to silence and impoverish persons that would not fight for his underground counterfeit army. Persons playing games with brain XXX logos learned how to defeat perverse, uncouth oppressors. The gateway had a peace arch monument with some of the original metal used on the archway from the 1800s. Job 1:12, 21. 1:22.

Job 3:19.

This was really a place even a feeble mortal alcoholic could tour and play in to restore their ripped-apart life.

The crew often rested after work in the clay guesthouses with elk bone fencing (Job 10, 27:16, 10) built around the midway park for the people of that neighborhood and their own visitors. Everyone was equal there. They almost had couples from every country. One woman from India, aged seventy-five, married a man from Italy, aged twenty-eight. They had the most respected friendship. Jealousy was crushed by natural shame. No one was alone or left helpless on chore day Monday.

Job 12:18

There was a relay each year in the midway park for the staff. Anyone could be a guest. They did not need a member's card. The staff would win gifts and would compete to win a custom-designed belt. Later would be a fashion show and a new game demo. It was a fun day with no tears or bruising, unlike the Valentine's Day historical tour and banquet, where tears were bottled and gifts of servitude awarded. Job 22:15, 27 Job 41

Job 11:16, 12:4, 12, 13:2, 9, 10 17:3 18:3* The season's gates shall open as proper toll is presented from one's way fair collection, which are indeed totem key tokens.

Job 22:2

Job 22:12

Job 25:2

26:21, Job 28*+

Wise kings will surely kiss the rising sun at Burger King that is constructed as a midway palace. Praise will be sung every time a game is won. As said in psalms, all will be judged, trialed, gifted. As the Lord endures forever and his judgment throne is prepared, and the Lord is refuge for the oppressed. The midway park was prepared as the dew ripened the budding cherry trees after a gentle, fragrant, pleasant, cheerful musical wind shaped the walkways of the grounds.

At the end of the trail, one's destiny map was earned. For a two-sided coin, a sun-kissed wet stone with a watermark or moonstones with etchings or a pouch for traders to carry treasures or pouches with roots and spices with a medallion or moon-phase crest from the massage parlor. Other trade items included houseware novelty from a home-sale network for singles like Art Deco ice cubes, table settings, and other custom-designed candy or dainty for a holiday or birthday party or media event. There were no game-land wizards to hex anyone economically as that would inevitably disadvantage them.

They held a lantern meeting to determine how to adjure the decision to select a new fish boat captain in charge of youth education. There was too much poverty and inactivity around the premillennium pools that were constructed with the illegal wages procured from after-hours swindling shindigs at popular casinos attacked by black arts gurus. Car aerials were mangled as adolescent sheep without a shepherd roamed ravaged by evil leasing lords that unfairly priced admiration. How to admonish under lords for their rip-offs and perverse oppression games was still just mused and tossed like a spin the bottle or dice game at an illegal hockey club or slum grove stable with no aesthetic value. Ad lib school plays and farmers' markets were illegally pirated, and few could enjoy customs of good cheer well adorned.

It was too often considered an adventure to give unruly advantage to under lords that had no courtesy. J-societies adversaries had looted many village alcoves from one metropolis to the next, illegally soliciting illegal trade vetoes and wars against fair-trade forms and people's press-construction projects. The aerodynamic charts of outdoor music festivals needed to be published with an advertised rating chart the public could respond to.

With afflatus, all on tour at the expo should excel so the moral benefit of the grounds ways was improved. Any afield needed better advice, not electronic tethering, so trade systems were tarnished and discontinued in remote areas where they were needed. Security sabotage had to be challenged. Electronic intelligence scripts from incriptions had to be reviewed so all citizens had their fair right to freedom of mobility and free assembly guaranteed. The torch to perfect city planning was lit so everyone was guaranteed satisfaction in all walks of life.

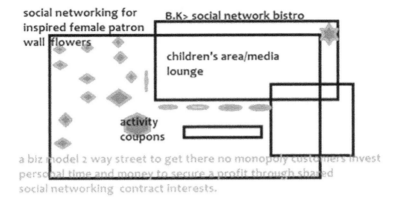

The way to freedom had to be written in the alabaster walkway. Agency scribes were out in their labs to make certain all agrarian citizens were equally respected. The most agile received the same hourly wage, but received extra for an embellished journal report entry. Some wrote they believed that Alchemy, the transgender pirate who was dubbed Script-Girl at the midway theater, had a vicious plan to infect the alderman with a rabies bite. Many mob members were following the alderman with plans to lunge attacks. He grew alfalfa for the math and applied science faculty banquets, and many did not believe or trust his ailment airy menu would justify the means of service. They wanted to elect a new water bearer proven trustworthy. So they removed the tom masks and trophy cups from the crest room. A place to reallocate them had not yet been decided justly, so they were buried beside the railway tracks until someone concerned enough went to get the map to relocate them.

They were not to be left in the massage parlor's private lounge for a wrest or gamble. That was considered an all right, fair move. The entire faculty boards of the transport services alma mater collective were in ambidextrous agreement. They then pledged allegiance to fair-weather amateur arts boards without any altruism to light. There were no put-forward altercations.

There was one man altogether amazed. No ambush to steal the keys to the map box had yet occurred. His allegro portrait was in midnight-alto color. The verse had to be performed to get the key and the map altogether as the music was in mind as the cups were placed in the burial pit where there was a magnetic alveolus to indicate the distance from the edge of the school ground where the treasured cups could be found.

Some teams might try to amalgamate to alter the altimeter markings to show where the location is by overland directives. An Amazon pirate could amass an army of apoliticals. It was expected that would wager tricks and guessing games as they could not follow the rules as monopoly could rake in more profit. The cash and token barter factors had to be eliminated somehow, or embittering tragic vexatious war would be priced for many moons, he determined. Aluminum tokens with engravings that fit into the map somehow might need to be used to end the monopoly scams. The ambitious ambassador would have to be summonsed to calibrate the tools for the expedition. A key the amber map would thus need. Everyone could view this on the twenty-seventh day of fall. That is when all amalgamation considerations would be signed. All the amenable would attend in their calling profile group designed to ameliorate the college's social networking forums. The flowers engraved into the amethysts were a games map. On Minigolf Mondays, anyone could enjoy some Coke double stackers and a Bike deli side order at the minigolf club if they did not want shooters at the booze hounds byway bowl arena. Burger Palace had a pavilion that had the most food court business. There were other novelties of tradition to consider at times when entering the social networking arena. To aver monopoly porosity in play tactics, dreams people submitted for review and analysis were fashioned as key tokens, credit icons, or symbols, and that made social networking through condo and apartment network modems allot more interesting as well by considering their meaning and with a special prayer or scripture affimation such as the scripture:

Psalm 9:18 for the needy shall not always be forgotten: 9:20

The company could amortize all the amorous through the social networking platform. That was the most exciting new policy established in the ultra-hi-tech unit that had automatic dispensary so organized, there were no garbage or toss-over concerns ever. There were sales record anecdotes posted on the walls, and information modems could be read on location from time to time to keep staff holding in mind all they had to do and talk about to maintain efficiency standards through the day. All staff acceded to plans to inure/ annul any garbage disposal systems.

The new system was an amusement with instruction and information anagrams. On Friday, many came with their anchor pass, which guaranteed them the special fish service they considered anew in their family journal anniversary annuls. They kept fish night stickers and trivia card games in their family journal, which talked about books they shared with friends when they were visiting. They also had a musical fish toy that they treasured as a table piece for their prayer banquet meetings. Ancestry records were important in every Friday fish fan's home. Everyone part of the group had an anklet with theme charms that were blessed in the name of holy mission angels and angels that were the guardians of the ocean, sea, and their respective vessels.

Dangling shrimp were the contribution of drunken, vain priests some worshiped as charismatic inspiration.

Fishing boat anthems were sung from the anthology collection after grace. It was their tradition to say grace at the end of the meal, not before service or breaking of bread, whether served prior to the meal or thereafter.

Apostles of the church brought Friday fish meals to all the apartment dwellers that would sign up for home Bible study groups through their conservationist ad mail system for the city. Not too many seemed antisocial. It was their bound duty to apace apathy as antipasto heated on the anthracite burner with the antebellum seal. It was from an era that began long before aerial mangling became a trendy mass social control mechanism. At staff meetings before the agenda was read, there was a study of trendy aphorism to apiece. The study taught sales strategy. Any in use with an apostrophe were the sayings customers used by their own choice to be popular with their friends there. At the end of the meeting, there was a discussion and slide show, if available, that showed the most popular apparel at that venue. These shorts would become promotional spots at the salons where staff were attended to, where they had membership. And they would be used as an end-of-the-year video montage for the Customer Appreciation Day ceremony. Musk arias helped the apprentice workers plan time management schedules effectively so all had a comfortable efficient environment to work in. Managers could appoint helpers if ever applicable. The best managers were applauded for the helps they assigned. A good match was often a good make. Staff were encouraged to keep an appetite log to share with sales customs review staff present at staff meetings in the accommodations with every convenient appliance and a clock-approved contract.

At the end of any day, the shift manager would apportion any menu suggestions. Apposite helpers that appreciated the rending customs always made a good apprentice. Once named, they were assistants to the manager at arable sporty arbors as they had artistic aptitude to arbitrate between the customs of each team.

One summer, a rogue skate club sortie took up to driving from one town to the next to cause some trade competition hurdles to become a vexation. The bunch would refuse to leave at closing time. They sometimes lit up smokes to frighten the staff; they would dump trash in the park lot and would spread around gang-war gossip in the park lots where they met to propose rumbles and duels. They were from a small town where their local bar closed because of the new law that put a ban on selling tobacco there. They knew that students against drunk driving had meetings at Burger Palace, and they took to showing up to meetings to harass the students. Some were robbed. When the attacks escalated, the throng of them began to steal Burger Palace art, resell it at taverns, or vandalize the frames and backs and dump it in the middle of the road saying it was a protest against all fuel distribution companies that were a biohazard. They claimed they had to create obstacles so fuel consumption was reduced. Yet the same odd fellows could be found drag-strip racing anywhere there were no radars, lasers, or cameras to record vehicle speed.

One person that organized some of the races started a covert operation against Burger Palace staff one stormy evening.

He started going to the SADD meetings there to meet one of the employees that was promoting the programmer. He was a sweet talker, and he seduced her. They began dating. He spoiled her quite noticeably then. He began to take her to lots of parties where he said they together would do more SADD promotions.

However, at the party, there was a lot of heavy-lane trafficking going on. Young boys and girls were working as private dancers and prostitutes at that house party spot. They drank way over the limit regularly. They put extra charges on the drinks and meals available sometimes. When the Burger Palace employee refused to return there and refused to kiss her new boyfriend, there his secret gang stole her car, vandalized it, and dumped it in the park lot to let the whole town know this was territory they were planning to take over, and they would not stop the bartering or merchandizing of women there. Their attack spread from SADD to Love Lives Here. And at that time, house party activity could not be regulated or even reported without severe retaliation. More technologically advanced car security systems were needed in the area, and more fair-trade groups needed support from one home to the next where drag-strip races were fund-raisers for red-lettering campaigns.

Trying to get SADD members addicted to outproofed black market alcohol was certainly no proper way to try to legalize drugs, pot, or spas with an escort club for home-care clientele. It was no easy challenge. And trafficking cartels were against the sale of red-card phone service download apps because the money to regulate sexual or other services offered at a house party or privatized race club would be taxed, and that would reduce the number of regular customer transactions considerably. Broadcasters, however, took on the challenge to some extent.

At some condo parks, they now had pavilions that served only Burger Palace pizza burgers. If you were a fan, you could order personalized Bike novelty items and get a portrait photo for a frame and a fan club card with your favorite saying and Bike cheer embossed. If you wanted to hang out in that park, job fair pavilions were open twenty-four hours at the midway concession stands. At this park, there was a drive-through concourse open twenty-four hours. There was a train station café there with a radio tower.

This café was the host of all participating events promoted and suggested and that the majority voted for in the city and in the various membership category groups. Participating groups supported SADD agendas. You could become a member of the radio station's fair-trade forum station and gallery. There was a broadcast history museum in the lobby. The children's park had scheduled events until 10:00 p.m. and was electronically under surveillance twenty-four hours. The group mandate was to get all house party groups to support participating events as part of the SADD agenda.

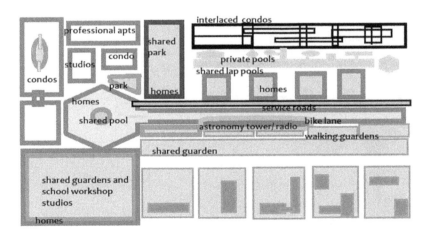

Some students started to put home-shopping club-member stickers on their cars with their SADD ID numbers. The stickers had a gap's bar code Burger Palace Coffee club member stickers were also distributed with an SADD support logo and saying or quote. More persons also installed minicams in their cars that would record any break-in activity on the neighborhood watch website. There was hope that would deter any black-label car-rustling activity.

The Official Games Menue

Firstly, a game app taught you how to invest in Burger Palace and related projects. TransCanada Corporation and crops so that as a customer, you also could be a dividend earner or cup holder. There were many types of games and genres of them: social networking, educational, travel club networking, farmers market logo, trivia, IQ, velocity, fantasy art, and also commercial games where the game was about creating a character to build Burger Kings and trade Burger Palace property. Also, you could generate a teen club event to host or sports event with all social calendars illustrated and scenarios animated. You got a character fan club page for free. And you could enter a contest to win a spot doing an ad for Burger Palace with your computer-generated character that would draw more clients to your personalized custom fan art page.

Midway Garden Games

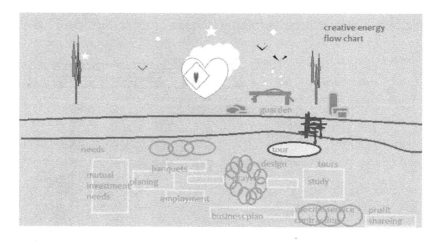

Everyone could profit from the concourse rounds at any location, even the apartment lobbies on free-range farms for transport staff that had a grocery deli at the lodge. Everything was OK there. You lived how you wanted to with a digital activity calendar. But no one could disseminate trafficking plans as there were lots of tours there. Burger Palace stamp collection art was trendy from time to time with general tour groups, not just campers. Some were on tours there to attend lodge events. The biz resource center scheduled for the poor that needed one. The lumber illusion art showing how the building came to be constructed was also popular. There was also a 3-D art exhibition and a toy art museum and new product development forum at this location. At the book fair, Burger Palace storybook trades were a main attraction every year. This was also where the railway history society held public meetings, so any staff that used BK for lunch would often stay an extra day for the trade fair.

The free-range farm lodge also invited tourism clubs to review campsite maps. They could contribute to at least one of seven farmers' market investment group projects. These projects included learning to play games so they could earn coupons with hunting, gathering, farming, fishing, and logo activities. On Chicken night, soda was free. The outdoor events were quite entertaining under the Burger Palace canopy tree. People could play checkers with miniburgers. They won fridge magnets and coupons, and the points system was graduated so there was more than one prize to win before the end of the game. There were also some places to interact with the acrobats if you had interest as you went on a complete grounds tour.

All the checkpoints had social networking ads. All the grounds apartments also had social networking modems to program electronic zodiac activity just like the city-apartments part of the subway metropolis. One of the most popular events at the free-range farm was the love train graffiti festival put on for singles after the gala. There they could take a train back in history to problem-solve ending war, poverty, casting by learning how to participate in a miracle play event. When they returned, if they wanted to, they could continue to attend auto-debit management seminars that were hosted to encourage the insurrection of an economic system that did not allow anyone to collect debt at anytime. Meaning that if you went on vacation to watch car races and eat burgers, the trip and each visit to the restaurant had to somehow pay for itself. Interactive business model construction education was part of the social networking plan. People from all over the world came to the auto-credit fair on the free-range farm to learn how to build a debt-free economy in their community through the corner store at the end of their street in a park, through residential ad mail, through their apartment lobby.

The same could be learned at the Burger Palace subway gallery for just the flip of a coin or gateway token. The first lesson you learned at seminars was to not ever kill the right to free speech, the bill or the act. The most seminars were hosted at a Burger Palace made in Russia by teens before they graduated from high school. They learned how to construct a building to work on in their industrial arts class. They invested savings into their new building. They also hosted social networking education seminars when persons visited them that were on a bus tour with a tour guide for professional development presentations. The trips were often chaperoned as many were young students. Burger Palace game shows also became popular on Russian prime time T.V. And the Burger Palace café in the broadcast station lobby/gallery was always busy.

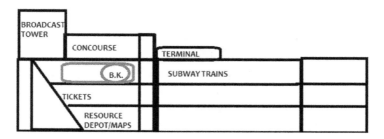

Broadcast Services Calendar

Each month of ascribed activity is presented to support the three Christian holy festivals described in the Bible as righteous custom to abide in. Each month, a census committee is created to make certain all poverty problems are judged and the cause of poverty is eliminated to make certain all residents have an activity calendar that is personalized so each individual enjoys the peace and good comfort they personally desire.

April: ecology education and interactive art, video rental sales
May: emergency preparedness drill video promotions, mine history exhibitions
June: applied sciences exhibition and new art education book releases
July: music festival, health and beauty, spa and sport promotions
August: gallery of light and architecture mixed media arts tourism club meetings (obscene, offensive, and illegal trade blocks all removed)
September: family reunions, fashion shows, antipoverty drives, festival to unite soul mates
October: creation animations, fair-trade festivals begin
November: underground society tours
December: charity galas, social networking seminars
January: astronomy promotions
February: electronica festival

March: festival of color, gem trading so none are lacking, single men
              serve all single women in the community, friendship-circle
              treaties are signed, fair-trade book club and ad mail kit
              promotions and official service package presentations, people's
              choice awards, people's press elections

Personal astrology calendars, digital dominoes, games, and charismatic
event planners with personalized social networking schedulers are all astute
promotions for event planners and any citizen with a seminar suggestion to
consider. The study of astronomy is not an atheist science. Gen. 1:14 Every
moment in time has meaning and value. Baccalaureate charity auction
staff avow each year thus to publish their professional autobiography in
magazine-form and share it out. Every employee should do the same. That
way, no one is baffled or oppressed.

And all people discuss what they each plan to do to end poverty
problems without any mica-mac-patty-whack balderdash crimes or raves.
People that want to work on the same project must thus be guaranteed
free assembly, not any backhanded backgammon to barter project-backing
offers. All badinage from fair ground to antique car show to rodeo
to stunt show to drive-through to school picnic must be licensed. The
schedule is printed as an addendum to one's colors associate card, client
card, color-coded citizenship card/event passport. Even the small talk of
shoeshiners at the bank is recorded from the evening on the employee's
trademarked service-bandeau from the fair-trade agribition. Games fairs
were a much better draw than a banjo bandwagon because the bandmaster
was better able to prevent raves, swapping scams, etc.

The baron outlawed roving barbiturate bards, but alas, illegal
competitions were illegally wagered. There was now an art fair to present
fantasy portraits of burger palace barmaids distributing health bars instead
of beer and cigarettes and a billboard to present the social concerns or
any single woman looking for a spouse. The burger palace was for singles
only. Singles owned it cooperatively, and the city council made certain
the programmers were administered lawfully without McBurger Baron
barratry and basket swapping so not every citizen was guaranteed their
basic rights. So some people thought more funds should be raised to build
more Burger Palace emporiums in Iraq, where married women did not
have their rights guaranteed. That would teach young people to act more
appropriately. Burger Baron missionaries put an end to all bar brawls in
some communities where the mellow-yellow Love Lives Here gurus failed

when they went through peace-walk ceremonies from one tavern to the next. Spas run by men for women in Burger Baron towns were a real success, some thought, because they guaranteed women had employment in any applied science group; they promoted local art most effectively. However, some thought that Burger Palace would be better for the people of Iraq and there could be a farmers' market with equality campaign bazaar pavilions to make sure no man was cruel to his wife and was a proper distributor of all alimentary benefit.

This might quell bawdy battalion brawlers bartering farm management contracts and attacking art co-ops for singles and collectives that needed mandatory support to end unemployment strife. Service of bread is to always be lawful and never oppressive or stifling or ritualistic or leasing. A new commission to tour beadles through Iraq's public festival venues/ taverns to make certain no one was lacking any service or treaty custom had to be established. And bean sale logos had to be illustrated in more detail so all had an agenda to follow as a law-abiding consumer. All bean fields were adoption agencies, and antiauto credit factions solicited since at least 1967 were illegal, and many civilians were illegally abused, segregated, uprooted, tortured, enslaved, forced, or even strangled into poverty. Compensation claims were never properly reviewed. Employment futures programs had to change all over the world. Guarantees had to be guaranteed, and gold seals could never be tarnished. Thus, a few beadles would be setting up new beams and refurbished bearings at sandy-shore beacons where Burger Palaces would be constructed with a hydraulic midway resort. Burger Palace would then sell chili in a World Youth Day mug. The fish menu would also increase.

People's Republic supporters began to sign contracts worldwide. People could now bask on the beach and enjoy shellfish salads from Burger Palace. In these areas now, some sport-plea stadiums now had an interactive sports network for singles. Basswood was carved at every entranceway to make certain fair-trade regulations were observed. A few new age business professionals decided their Burger Palace would replace the local sport lounge that served alcohol. And there would be a menu and a nonalcoholic beverage lounge for singles. There would be also a Burger Palace bus on the dial-a-bus route and a Burger Palace limo that could pick up clients or drive them home. The taxi service would be networked and would be a carpool service to home sales or preferred customer. sales party club members. The lobby was custom designed with the ten commands, a fair-trade crest, and savannah equality totem engraved on the left wood column. The right column was crushed marble and recycled metals. Very old-fashioned-style carriages could deliver orders to your home, and each cart had Internet to show what orders were assigned on a digital delivery map. The digital delivery maps had visual weather report markers and trivia information at milestones that were dated. The land survey commission approved of the maps.

In other areas, any BK promotion was ignored because the only social activity there was created at the bathometry disco with full-service spas, rental rooms, and a bar open twenty-four hours at the highest room in the tower above the cleft. All foods served there were packaged with tantric art symbols. There was no other kind of packaging allowed in the area. It was not legal to swim in Burger Palace costumes there.

In other communities where the seafood menu was expanding, it became custom for fashion show contestants to dress as a Burger King to lead the fashion show parade and procession through pools with social club activities, hotel pools where fashion shows were hosted, private party pools, and regatta galas. At the end of the parade, only one king was voted most fashionable at each location. The most popular king won some money to invest in his future fashion career. An animated 3-D film about the event was also on a global tour.

Training Staff to Entertain

It was sometimes a difficult task because some were not inclined to make a contract to study dictionaries daily, be musical, talk much at fashion shows, and learn how to smile to promote vegetarian burgers, or learn how to be part of a comedy show for staff party events or new product demonstrations. Most staff in rural/small town locations were not interested in learning sales routines. Some of the elite were in cliques that would sell burgers at private house parties that students found most popular. They would do stunts and even magic tricks with the burgers they brought to the parties with them. The parties were at hotels where they worked or traveled with a sport team or with swimming or drinking buddies most often. They often lacked professional finesse desired, but they were most popular events. But some staff started to wear fancy burger promo shirts and hats wherever they went, just to get the company more attention. They also would become a draw or attraction then.

The fashion gimmicks sometimes got more basketball players and soccer players in for a meal after a game. It became a routine for the local soccer players at the leisure programmers to play a game, grab a quick meal, then cruise around town, check out a party, and play games with the meal deal toys in a magical sort of way. A few started to wear wigs to go out to Burger Palace events. These sorts were armchair comedians that wished they were famous but could never afford to be. They went to the Burger King outlets with cage wrestling on the pt. They would cheer when their favorite Burger Palace ads were on the pt., usually the one with mountain climbers hiking to a high-cliff mansion-style Burger King with tree house-style cottages around the waterslide park. Computer animation effects got the loudest cheers and yahoos. Most times, they were out bantering and setting up a battalion of cattle-crowing session followers. Not one of them ever washed their beards with beer shampoo.

They always attended the biannual WWF meetings at Burger Palace, and they always agreed to do a Burger Palace biz lunch there at least once a month, unless a tour prevented that in some way. At these meetings, they would review a bibliography study the lead wrestler wanted to discuss. At this time, many from the bivouac fields would come into town for lunches. The blue-collar crowd was around then, but they would do takeout if the tables were full. The blue-chip clients were there only on holidays or evenings before curfew hour was set. During bivouac season, they even got some clients that were quite regular from the boardwalk boardinghouses. The workers wanted an evening out, and it was a nice walk there for tourists. Also, there were some bouillabaisse and chili promo entertainment there as advertised on the boulevards and at the USA borders. On the big billboards were dancers and other characters with a bouquet and candy package.

Across the border you could find many that would race all hours to get to the bough in the Burger Palace park lot first. Some of the racers with flags said it was testosterone that made them fight to see the pretty girl at the order window first. Others thought it was a political game or monopoly without much moral thought to it at all. Like a clan war or bourgeois bounder cap war that put an unfair edge on job contract bidding bouts. To prevent that, some considered they would have a company social affairs director transport workers to events at local churches when they had time off together. The program had to be optional though. At present, some managers would not conform to the imposed regulation of organized religion and would refute and confront the confuted organized agenda proposed or imposed. When a job contract bid was solicited, all concerned needed a contract of fair commodious commitment. When a contract to sell more vegetarian burgers was proposed, staff that could teach workers how to smile, offer, and serve vegetarian burgers were needed. When staff needed better housing arrangements, then commonwealth realty development collectives were needed so unification was tangible reality. A commodore had to be assigned to replicate, reprimand, adjudicate, or repartee any contrived or incidental nuisance.

There was lots of contention concerning why organized church groups or factions congregated in parks without any conglomerate structure or twenty-four-hour business clubs established to guarantee personal and civil security. Some of the tours really seemed to support contraband hate crimes. So the building of golf clubs to dampen and quell the gracious behavior was not quality Methodism. Burger King palaces with ecotourism and participation concourses thus had to be established in parks all over the world, in the USA, in Mexico, in Iraq, and also other commonwealth tourism destinations on the agenda. Mob monopoly had to be indefinitely quelled, particularly in the Iraq region. In other areas, twenty-four-hour charismatic diner theater clubs with people's press copyright options could be an option to illegal corduroy discos, pantomime clubs, speakeasy and booze billet bars, and cloth-box tarot trail venues. Otherwise, some truth seekers might enjoy a free buffet at the Cooper's ice festival café where cookies were sold to raise funds for antipoverty projects. Also, their biotecture co-op would do custom catering by request. Any holiday event or birthday or other promotion or special day to celebrate could be accommodated.

Cork and/or coral centerpieces were available in the gift shop for a preferred donation of forty dollars and no less than five dollars. Poetry club members also could sign up for pizza delivery on call or the dial-a-prayer custom-order menu. They maintained holistic service customs. After each meal were music, poetry, conversation, future planning, praise and thanks, prayer, investment counseling, relaxation session, and tea service with accompaniment. Cordial tea service could include other sales promotions or solicitation. It was a time that vegetarian burger coupons could be solicited. Chameleon mimics could not plan or organize investment strategy rip-offs. One of the most interesting centerpieces was a cornucopia with a digital art screen in the center of the largest regional presentation of corolla that were local. Some of the videos were dance vignettes by mimes in fur costumes. It was entertaining comedy. There were other more amusing scenes also by illusion and midway artists and multicultural poets. Also, faith healers had a series of promotions to help along the interactive counseling and advisement process. All by law need and must have good comfort and good cheer (Gen. 44:15, 34:16, 44:1, Ex 18:21, 18:19). Thus, every bank must manage a census so no single client is lacking, as must every church and professional and cultural and sport and consumer association or warehouse club.

3

Typical Warehouse Club Models

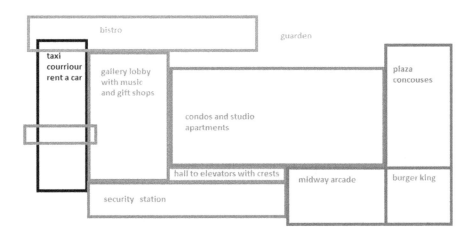

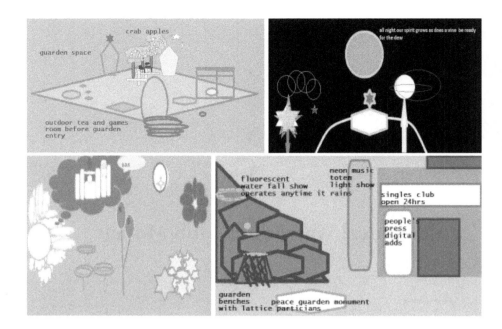

Petition   *July 4.docx*
PETITION   *July 6.docx*
101 nonalcoholic beveredges.docx

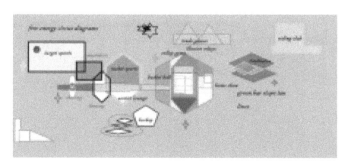

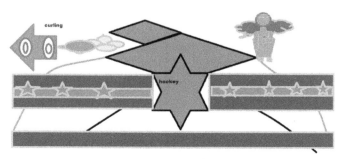

It was also noted that many people since the World Trade Center was first constructed have contested against the fast-food business, complaining that snack food service customs need a holistic edge and that it must be law to serve only solid meal combinations and nothing less. On PTA day, a vote must be held. Ecoculture sport labs seemed to have more industrious potential than new age conservative Christian discos (*1 Cor. 1:13*) There have been debates about how to construct a business venue with a holistic policy to make sure that all needs of the staff are met and all employees enjoy good cheer and good comfort for their term of employment.

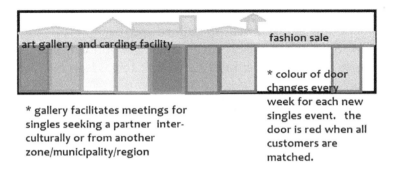

* gallery facilitates meetings for singles seeking a partner inter-culturally or from another zone/municipality/region

* colour of door changes every week for each new singles event. the door is red when all customers are matched.

(*1 Cor. 6:2-3, 11, 14, 17, 20, 6:4*) God shall raise up all with spirit to build so none are defrauded.

(*1 Cor. 7:5*) In times past, many were wrongly treated for more than ten days, more than three years, more than seven years, more than ten years. Mobs that were not fair players monopolized the labor contracting and publishing illustrations industry for illegal gains so holistic fair-trade contracts and investment plans could not be signed in the year 2000, and gross oppression continued illegally beyond the 2010 Olympic Games. (*1 Cor. 8:7*) It must be upheld law that food-service customs are not idealistic or based on policy of evil lease or policy of casting or any class system or illegal wrestling competition or beauty contest or contest of prejudicial construct. Food service must be 100 percent nourishing spiritually, physically, educationally, aesthetically, and to be sure socially and to prosper the benefit of the esteemed value of nourishments. (*1 Cor. 8:13*.) So we do not need to gamble before any meal or try to wrestle away rights before any meal or to fight for the right to party and serve or entertain at a food-services venue. Wrestling to be Water Bearer and monopolize one's search for a helpmate is not legal custom either.

(*1 Cor. 7:29.*)

This scripture is best for study if ye decide to be a café manager or water bearer that none be defrauded and all have good cheer and satisfaction by lawful custom. But I say, brethren, the time is short. It remaineth that both they that have wives be as though they had none. Thus, no marriage may be a contract of leasing or to suggest any caste system be imposed. Some social policy in past years have not been true, just, and useful to anyone. It has been idealistic and corrupt. Persons harmed by such unlawfulness must be awarded overdue compensations. That process can be accomplished through social networking education modem installation.

Social networking polls are the same as census polls, designed to make certain no person is oppressed, defrauded, set back at any time in the year (*1 Cor. 8:12*) If a weak consciousness is wounded, yea sin. Social networking polls should be conducted weekly and at least four times each year.

1 Cor. 9:1

9:1-5. 6.

1 Cor. 9:7

So if all customers part of a niche dinner club with a social network invest in that venue for a dividend return, they each get a section of garden to plant, part of an acreage, or part of a garden on the roof investors choice programmer. (*1 Cor. 9:11*) Sow what is spiritual. Let no liberty become any stumbling block.

the most simple form of a socialized co-op cafe.
- a tree-house style craft covy warehouse. All members get a free meal daily, a weekly pay deposit for craft or other art works done. the club has commercial sport event$,dateline web & social network so all members have a chapperoned date service.

Why do we need professional chaperones?

Even before the 2011 Olympics, schedules were sabotaged by redneck twisted sister gooks and sorcery game impresarios. All citizens needed monitored premarital counseling services to prevent economic collapse due to rivalry and oppressive segregation scams and illegal job marketing competitions by privatized brothels, autocrats, dictators, or underground oligarchs. We need a communications server that unites persons with same concerns and goals. No one should be segregated, oppressed, manipulated, impoverished, and made friendless or a target of ridicule. Burger Palace dance party mix music was against the hip-hop roller coaster horror craze and new age rap beats.

General Policy to Serve Single Female Customers and Mandate of Stewardship to Single Female Employees

1 Cor. 9:10 Plough in hope. Meaning as you work through the day, you should not be trying to subjugate others that share your work space. You should make your routines to be equitable so that persons learn how to be of mutual benefit to other workers so that they are better service attendants, ready to efficiently serve to meet clientele expectations.

1 Cor. 9:5 Electronica music should be positive moral encouragement so all employees have knowledge on how to take the lead in any social situation and act as a lawful citizen.

1 Cor. 8:13 Observed.

Single women should be served an additional appetizers menu that is in season.

Single men should be served a separate side orders menu that is illustrated.

1 Cor. 9:4 Consider all of what it means in menu design planning that we have power to eat and drink.

9:24 God and his angels bless the menu plans of twenty-four hour stewardship venues. 1 Cor. 15:25, 26

What is a man of good dessert? What is the purpose of a daily double dessert? 1 Cor. 10:17, 11:22, 12:4

1 core 7:27-31.

7:35 This is spoken so all client investors may profit. 1 Cor. 14:33

Female staff receives the same meal benefit plans and specials offered as customers do.

Also, the female staff receives coupons for home spa service on their regular days off (1 Cor. 9:19) during their menstruation cycle. These are paid days off for all staff.

The male staff may request holiday time where they have a personal contract stating they have duty of care (1 Cor. 7:34, 35, 9:12) or whereby they need time for personal refreshments (1 Cor. 11:32-34).

1 Cor. 12:31.

1 Cor. 15:28-58

Marketing Strategy

The first business concern for the majority was to make sure that all SADD members had current promotions. Next was to make certain all Love Lives Here had current Burger Palace biz lunch offers and current passport membership kit profiles and updates. Ads could also be posted at Weight Watchers and other health points regulation program stations. Each station is thus color-coded to indicate what social behavior trends were customized. Some regions had multilevel marketing competition strategies that seemed a bit roughish. It began where cars were sold and all the staff said, "Have a nice day" with the same tone that you would expect when they noticed the fragrance of the soap you used. It was like anyone should be guaranteed a good day because they were brand conscious and noticed the colors of the sunrise in a significant way. How to be brand conscious though became debated as though it could be just a new gambling system to capitalize on.

Cars were not only sold to persons with an appointment and an employee card and key pass number. They were sold by the tone or tint of karma the buyer expressed. More accurately stated in accounting project folders these, they were sold where the buyer showed their war paint colors. Some registered mine corps though intended to continue the conveyance of privately authorized, colorized premium-rate options and were strictly unconventional. Not everyone opted to buy yellow cars with Love Lives Here logo windows to quell any bar-war issues. It was agreeable to do just that though.

Other marketers sold promotions to persons with flags on their cars. Some had flags to advertise their personal admiration of a famous racetrack, campsite, resort, sport team, church, or environmental campaign.

Sales campaigns were tagged, meaning that the base color was the same as the color of car the customer had. And logos in that color car sale agents assigned to promo spots. Also, the customers would receive custom marketing tickets that were designated by the rime then of their license plate. After the client's car exterior was cleaned, the attendants would put promo pigs under the windshield of the car. Most would subscribe to phone info downloads though. Marketing and business students though would still hand deliver customized flyer kits from time to time. Marketing education was available in the opening hours before a shift started, at lunch, on breaks, after staff meetings, on scheduled seminar dates, and while the employee waited for their salon or spa appointment. Massage sessions were training pep talk sessions. Pep talks got staff idling, ready to drive at the pace reality marked out.

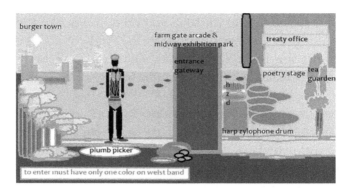

Fair-Trade Week

Cars with Go Green Canada flags, Burger Palace toy land flags, biofuel industry promotion flags, and magnetic stickers to remind car passengers to recycle were lined up to get to the BK drive-through window. Some people were listening to audiobooks on their MP3 player. Burger King toy characters were talking about how to keep the earth green and free of any trash footprints. All the music tracks were made with musical instruments made from recycled materials. Most of the customers were using the coupons that came with the fair-trade triathlon ticket packages. Many special events now came with fluorescent Burger Palace coupons. Most schools were in agreement that their games promotion magazines decreased dropout rates and failures. Their social events were good for public morale and improved socialization and social networking, so there was less poverty and less street gang and drag-strip race crime that was deconstructive, prejudicial, and economic strife and illegal rivalry.

It was important to note the following:

Seasonal customer services reporting seminars are important to attend to make sure all people have the social security they need, the good comfort, and good cheer they wish for so they can engage in conversations that are educational, profitable, and intellectually stimulating. Thus, singles are guaranteed by law. They have professional development support in their social environment also and from suitable chaperones. Thus, freedom of assembly is guaranteed, so none lack any good comfort or are in poverty. All singles need at least one nonalcoholic venue with free monthly professional development seminars put on by cooperative leaders. Singles with matching interests should be mailed tickets with the same table number.

Meetings could also be held at a green warehouse monthly at noon, Passover, harvest, and when employees called a meeting. The public could also submit contributions.

It would be nice if Burger Palace staff had a better housing plan. It was put forward. Condo-style apartments with deli catering services and professional development seminars at the leisure center convention room were liked. There could be entertainment venue for staff also with visits from mimes, stewards, program directors, entertainers, charismatic actors, magazine journalists, crafters, recycling firm reps, toy designers, product demonstrators, motivational speakers, system designers, maintenance workshop hosts, counselors, music therapists, masseurs, artists, mentalists, prayer custodians, professional seminar developers, and demonstrators. Web education for staff needed to present educational questions in web-letter form that would educate and teach prepaid staff to organize for work, as the job application test questions indicated there should be a list of professional development books and CDs staff may order. Guild tests done online can be encoded on the employee card for billing meals etc.

The customer services review and reporting seminars were available every year to any staff. A certificate was provided. They were optional and not mandatory. A video described how to report on the social life and circumstances of clients, how to report any mentioning about the condition of their vehicles or car service needs, how to report on the influence of stress or apparent illness, how to record purchase preferences of a customer, how to record favorable comments on the company blog, how to record sayings and comments and how they are valued, and how to record holiday comments. There were also seminars on carding security that could be attended.

Really, a security camera system with carding control should be installed so that each table number and the card number of the client is recorded on the bill. The camera can judge all that customers do, even events like "The client stuck gum under the table." A list of disorderly clients should be kept, and lists that detail their aberrant behaviors should be sent to social programming psychologists or mentalists that can modify their behavior. Client efficacy has to be maintained. When going over some of the comments in the customer suggestion box (which from time to time had love notes or gifts to a staff member), a few workers decided they should try to publish some new recipes for the clients. Maybe they would get a sales commission for it. Suggestions were herb butter beef slices and gravy. They might be a big sell at the Burger Palace that was a ski hill games resort where they sold Burger Palace brand earmuffs and Burger King crests and badges to school children that took trips there. Breaded beef strips, gravy tenders, a saucy tender grill buffet in a box, meatball stew, spicy chicken salad in a mug, cheese sauce and dry onion burger pouting with bacon bits and spicy crisps and mild salsa, smoky chicken and spaghetti in a mug, pasta in a mug, dry soup, pizza on the side, and specialty desserts. The regular menue there was the same daily and the same music played for every order served. The color themes on the ads are also a spark of interest for toys to be marketed at home sale parties. Home party kits can be bought at the deli with delivery services, and the customer newsletter would then put ads in for toy painters, play park attendants, party clowns, shoeshiners, and puppet show writers, also fashion critics and journalists. The magazines could have press and play or cutout Burger King toy game instructions and theater sets in them from time to time.

Later, after sunset, it was decided that meatball stew could be a new option for the serial about Burger Palace

Some scripts could be menu titles, and the cast could include comedians, staff party entertainers, staff hairstylists, aestheticians, masseurs, apron dusters, head office entertainment co-coordinators, and a toy sales rookie. And the young adult section could have ads for singles seeking friendship and romance after the game program and music CD tour news so even Burger Palace would have their own talent agency that would drive concertina staff from one location to the next for events. Elroy said he loved listening to music with light-up Burger Palace logos on his download player or headphone radio with Burger Palace stickers. He said the musicians and their slaves all seemed to be charismatic, but what romance was cooking for them, he wondered from time to time. For sure, it seemed some had been stewed or broiled. And he wondered why we should need sport club leathers anymore. He also thought that he did not need a school dance party anymore. Instead, there could be an end of the year job fair and treaty signing and auto club sale at Burger Palace. He even fantasized that in Alaska, a Burger Palace plaza would link underground transport services to global warming news station and king castle realty.

The communities in Alaska passed a law that all food or culinary arts or restaurant or catering venues, by law, had to serve balanced menu items, meaning that salad was only an optional side order and could not be ordered separately as every menu portion had to constitute a solid snack or meal even if it was not packaged by sellers or mosaic corporation. The law had to be abided the same way by every company in North America and every import network.

Sunset Rhythms to Mull and Create a De-stress Formula

It was the end of another long day. The cars were ribbons of the sunset light, and Al was tired. Ali dusted him off, and Lie gave his shoulders a rub down and served his evening meal. After grace, he asked, "Why does Caira yell angry-like sometimes? Some lady says she was almost cussed at for changing an order of fry to poutine." Was Caira trying to get America to cut down on salt in a rush? Was her tartness psychological in that way? Who had an art to test and trial her sore, vexed spirit? Someone wanted extra help or extra helpings, and that made her yell, caste, curse. Some people jeopardize them, so they do not have help and have to race around with nothing, so they have to beg in fear with no comfort. Why does she impose condemning ways?

Her rules to weigh judgment do not seem fair. They seem oligarchy. All are subjugated as inferior under the family head as supreme ruler and dictator, so she stops mincing like a dictator from a hustler set. She might attend a workshop on how to learn to communicate effectively and not be rude or self-inflicting so that working conditions can be improved. She needs to learn effective cooperation skills. She and others need effective time management planning seminars, effective motivational writing skills lessons to improve departmental efficiency and compatible scheduling, a seminar so she learns to ask the right questions. Everyone needs seminars on combating price-fixing scams, recycling system improvements, effective communication skills to make application for emergency child care services or parental leave.

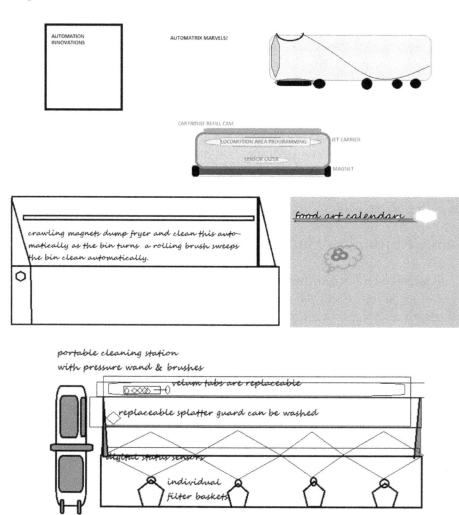

There would be new ads in this year's catalogue for employee stock, etc., and also the magazine for staff and quarterly newsletter. All seminars were customized and had registered certificate rewards.

There was also a special management course for staff wanting promotions at food court locations. Especially locations that animated dream art or art customers suggested. Some of the concourses had also Burger Palace or Burger Baron carts or carousels. They needed extra staff to keep taking the used cups to recycling bins and the slat bin refuse to the garb orator. Some of the staff were given gift certificates to spa seminars on how to manage negative low esteem, how to clarify facts, avoid customer arguments even when cursed until stressed, how to deal with oppressed caste members part of drug cartels, scalping or panhandling, how to subdue those that cuss to barter, how to try to enlighten the rude and degrading, how to judge those evasive to cause harm, how to deal with clients that smoke too much, how to cope when weary and dropping stock, how to deal with political assault, pushy violation razz, to disable customers with complaint of financial burdens, the politically naive.

If mall security needed upgrades, they had a corporate plan to deal with it and compensate for it even in times when people had to look for shelter from natural disaster in churches, schools, plazas, galleries, also socially ethical plazas and shopping concourse subways and networks. Some of the food court training videos showed staff how to distribute Bible society information as pruning the road to peace is necessary to sculpt security. We all should acknowledge God is king. All private school managers must strive to be the servants of God's angels. Pray, for God is the creator of all foundations for grace, peace, truth, charity, enlightenment, and mission to abolish all poverty so all have a pathway to secure relationships of promise and profit, good comfort, and good cheer. It is thought that as midways and theaters merge, all can be guaranteed a pathway to good cheer and good comfort. God is our master and holy teacher. All need guaranteed equality.

The most beautiful gallery I ever dreamed of was a long brick corridor with music that gave me a real appetite. I walked through the corridor, and I could see a great vision at the end of the hallway from the clouds. I loved the fragrant winds. I enjoyed seeing all the art posters on the wall.

There was a beautiful graffiti art garden for outdoor barbecues and a bike rodeo where staff could also celebrate the Festival of Colors while at work or home. It was the same condo complex. There were lots of game apps to play in that garden's LAN like it was a dreamworld. It was so cool, so beautiful to walk through the pulse of the charismatic music in the gallery full of Burger King scenery, paintings, and memorabilia.

What kind of people still went out for a meal sometimes?

The best consultants needed to be gathered to publish a more accurate fine-dining magazine with no sector barriers.

NIA?

I called out to Nia. She used to be a graphic artist, but now she never wore pink, at least not when she knew I would be aboard her team. It was not significant to me though. Nia was Nia, my loyal friend. I asked her why some people did not understand why it seemed that modern cafés had to be socialized. She said some were just rebels that did not like the system. They were competition addicts. She also said we did not need a rodeo anymore. It was too much of a risk. A cool rodeo on a mediocre day was just a dream. It never would be cool in the end, just a fiasco with a lot of complaints she did not want to hear about. And she was likely to get married to someone that believed the same way she did. She really thought any rodeo would only be asking for trouble of some sort. Nia and I did not drive the same kind of car. She made sure she bought one nothing like mine to make that statement solid as rock, steel, water, or anything on this earth.

But I still said it had to be that way though so that there was not a problem with welfare and industry collapse. Governments were responsible for the welfare of each resident just like the priests were to be. And business professionals also needed to serve clients from a holistic portal on the web to be sure there was no one lacking any comfort. That would be responsible astrology. Whether you wanted government in your zone or not, all had to play by the same rules equally fair to each individual.

Why socialize entertainment and vending venues? "When man is a fool, he needs education?"

He needs education.

He needs better travel guide education.

He needs better travel and finance information.

When in confusion, a hustle is not light to avoid a bustle.

If you liked games on communications networks, some of Euni's favorite players knew a game called the crime stoppers treaty solutions card game. If you landed on a crime in progress square, you drew cards to learn how to negotiate repentance. Euni said if we had a socialized venue games, in one way or another, we had to test that all members did abide a code of laws and rules to get comfortably acquainted. Thus, people talk to each other and not at each other. Communications services need to link people that share ideas and customs so there is peace and unification, no XXX dub poets just born to hack any system. But scholastic life was not just about games. It was about learning to make contract commitments to colleagues so that every student had an SADD-approved cachet and gift set for Couple's Day, and the graduation benefit scheduled the same day as the car show. Cabana sideshows with burlesque bordello brownies were not considered ethical. Persons without a cachet could earn one by participation in a social networking event or holistic sales networking presentment. Menu puzzles fit into calendar chips. Calendar chips could help anyone earn all the credit points they desired. Even if their only wish was to have a Burger Palace logo plays land in their own backyard.

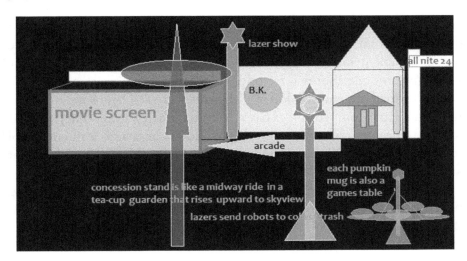

Communications services need to link people that share ideas and customs so there is peace and unification no XXX dub poets just born to hack any systems. Communications services need to link people that share ideas and customs so there is peace and unification no XXX dub poets just born to hack any systems.

Leon's perspective was a bit different. In the realm of the fast-food drive-through industry from a socialized and cultural perspective, all we participate in should generate income we needed—economic, social, intellectual, educational—so all was in balance. A basic income was an energy circle with a lot of vibrant colors. It was not a bad dynamics grid. We watched Euni, Nia, Reu, and Neon walk down the dusty street. It was, it seemed, the hottest day of the year! Not one hip-hop drag race anecdote was heard. Was life to begin or end if God was eternal? That was what Neon thought. It was his belief, not a magic trick from a disco down deadbeats' road. Neon also thought life ended when a girl turned a guy down for a date at specifically the baby blue eco-friendly gala that would be platformed at the senate club's arcade for students ready to apply for carding and fingerprinting. But some people thought it was called baby blue because students refused to buy hotel logos for a gas card credit. There would be maybe a few weddings after the gala where the light shows went on twenty-four hours because new life continued for a free sucker or a booklet of all the same coupons.

So Rue met Nia after school there. There they would play games. There they were game partners because after their school test scores were in their circle of numbers, and test score translations matched, so they agreed to date. It was a formal process with mathematical function, as it should be for sustainable living. Also, they really liked each other's shoes. They were something for the motto for world peace, they both really believed in. Also, they had the same color of game quest crest. They wanted to win from the game competition. That is why they had a crest. They wanted to win the games competition so they could get an award at their school reunion. They really wanted the prize because they liked each other a lot and believed the school system their parents voted for really did work!

Euni had a day off. She was fifteen and had her first job collecting tickets one or two days a week at the arcade club. She had benefits so that she could enjoy her day off with custom home spa and catering service, and she had a gym pass. She was in a class on management and how to be an effective social director, but all other staff had the same benefit provisions. Sometimes she was called Unice. Unice liked Neon because he was a philanthropist that saw the light shine through the darkness of the dark side. She believed he would overcome and remain on the straight road to peace even after his charity mission toast. When we all got to the bright lights that day, Nia said she'd rather skip. Rue, however, said for sure they all had to be at the gala though. It was their oath and responsibility. Nia did not kick at that but wanted to explore more first, saying the pre-gala fashion show was a drab and, unfortunately, not really of her taste. She figured the master of ceremonies held her cards wrong, and as she had done that, she would auction the MC's shoes before early retirement. After though, she was branded! Bad news! It was released. She was not worth an exchange replacement, not worth a smoothie service. Rue was disappointed with her. He made plans to talk to the stewardship council at school.

There was a lot of other stuff to do at the museum, science center, gym, leisure center, and park, stuff that kids could do to get away from the repetition of the mainstream education agenda and still receive credit for what they like to do with time off school. Even Christmas party comedy routines could make someone a bit wealthier than they were before. Even news documents, chats, or posts were worth credit points, as is a conversation with a hairdresser before work. Coupons were available and useful. A visit to the staff aesthetician was better than a free astrology reading sometimes. Rue really liked the fashion shows he had been to and had helped plan, but had some of Nia's plans been really bad news—competition, illegal journalism—to make sure mockers made someone feel cursed and torn when they entered into the square of public confrontation where they were given fame or misfortune? Why would it happen? What could it be all about? What was really wrong? Why was she so vague and abusive? Their master of ceremonies was for sure no wretch.

Rue was afraid that Nia might suggest they go somewhere not approved for students at this time, like a café, a bar, or even a Burger Palace games emporium where you could get lost in some addiction you did not need, it was assumed. That idea scared him a bit. He was afraid to buy her a Burger Palace friendship ring after school now, especially as she announced she was a dictator that had a mob following him to destroy his esteem. They sometimes went together using the club passport card. Their parents signed both their names and the names of four other friends. If the name was not on the card, it could not be used for any purchase. There was no cash. Children around there hang out all the time with their friends' Dads. it was not unusual. If you were friends with a classmate, you were friends with his dad too. So the friends and family pass was accepted. The establishment could be trusted. They had a staff dietitian referral service and other professional services for staff in the staff catalogue. The staff doctor could assign home care staff for any need, even the needs of children. Also, the staff doctor gave out home remedies, booklets, and information scratch cards to persons in need of ailment airy care—they were diagnostic strips that were used as a prescription. They were a good community network to use as a resource, not pretentious in any way.

After her shift, Nia decided on a walk in the park on the way past the midway and concessions to the leisure center. When they got to the park, she gave Rue a friendship gift she got from the fair-trade vigil held there. The gift to him said she wanted to get together at the Burger King art fair and wanted also to keep in touch as good friends after the end of the school term. They should be there for each other no matter what as friends! They enjoyed some homework assignments together and were on time and enjoyed lunchtime conversation and never made plans that were aversive or awesome. She wanted to be friends and wanted to continue as friends through the games network too, so it was decided that she did deserve a friendship ring and charm for a bracelet. Bracelets sold Mondays had participaction symbols, Tuesday friendship lockets were offered, Wednesday trades union crests and flags were marketed, Thursday game coin tokens were presented, Friday school mission icons were served, Saturday travel clubs presented their charms, Sunday charity seals were present for donations thus each day only certain types of bracelets were available for purchase.

4

The Engagement Party

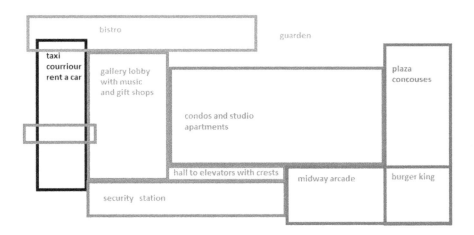

Scheduling a engagement party at a burger palace could be like living in a 3d paint by number scene you could make yourself.

Ret and Tina sold 3-D postcards in the lobby because they were engaged. They thought they'd see them there together every Thursday past 1:00 p.m. until they were entering their golden years and ready to have an anniversary reunion at Burger King. Ret and Tina made the leisure center look really cool, like the best place to be somehow, and they really did want to be there. The art gallery hosted free music video events daily ant 3pm. Every month there was a fashion show and poetry from the dream research institute. Rue was nervous they might be late for the gala, but he had set his watch alarm and the alarm in his electric car with hybrid bio-fuel cartridges. Nia was not too much annoyed by his nervousness.

Life at the new leisure center was not like fighting through the bramble of the YWCA that had become a sloven marsh.

Leisure centers had food courts and holistic massage clubs and pools for specific occasions, and activities had custom music made by DJs that were music therapists that worked with health counselors and advisors. At the new leisure center, some events had dress codes, clients had to present a biometric ID card that had all their skills and interests classed and coded and timed on their scan card so that all were guaranteed freedom of assembly. Each client thus has a schedule that is useful to them and customized. It is a mutual, legal, lawful agreement. Leisure participation credits would be added to their school course credits. Some games they did play taught them musical notes, so now they could get credit for what they learned after. With those points, they could access museum of natural and applied sciences tapes and answered trivia and attention-span questions. This was not like the games at warehouse clubs that socialized consumers, so they had support groups, Valentine's Day, and holiday socials and purchase power clubs and various investment education games. Jewelry had calendar and anniversary renewal themes. It was fun shopping and meeting people that liked to participate in product-demonstration trials with you. That was fun like at the midway arcades too.

Rue really wanted to be there before the gala, so he wanted to leave early to walk through the park. The leisure center was good because you never kept bumping into people you did not want to imagine or opposition you thought was a political waste of time with nothing of value to say. You were not forced to compete for popularity or social status points. You met people that filled out forms like you and had an organizational group number on their card. It had no silent war code like in some science fiction novels. Some people, though it cost an arm, believed that tattooing was the best service trade seal, and they even got one to trade circus toys and make some sort of statement about the voodoo chaos in shipping wars. Hip-hop after the library closes. Some nights, the leisure center or museum had film nights. If you did not like that, you could go to swim. The musical light show would indeed be brilliant. And on these occasions, controversy in social science was judged as philanthropists and ministers promoted group discussions, perspectives, and theologies, and sport therapists and cultural affairs directors had a duty to subdue any alcoholic ravers. Charismatic events were designed to resist mob hoodoo events. Modern conventional public facility design was more individual programming than group-rate perspective. Customer points of view became part of select choice groups' ratings that promoted organizational participation and even what type of candy should sell at the coiffeur salon. Anyone could go to the gala that would start soon. A coded organizational class card was not needed. There were machines for getting a club card open through so that persons could not be left behind from trade circle participation if they did not have one yet. Card users that evening could vote electronically to rate programmer activity and polls. He wanted to get there quickly. He was hungry and really wanted to test the programmer scores on the audience and rate his views of audience experience.

There was no grace ceremony. The oriental tourism and art auction buffet circuit was at its most ultimate low. Accountants were missing, bookings were cancelled, there were fights going on that had no logical explanation, a dictator that had uncouth policy was ripping everything apart.

Café managers sat in empty rooms, tears rolling down their faces, wondering where their next meal would come from as tomato crops failed, and many had thought they had to join hustler gangs to turn some kind of profit where there was no room to earn it. Promises were broken, and there was no one nearby to heal wounds or broken hearts.

There were no lights at the dance halls anymore, where the daring dangled charms that could be cutting war cry alarms. There were no more cushions to serve to mob numerologists custards. People followed a cursor to stay on the right path of the trails alongside Peace River where now the dapper never did prance through field or theater to dare habberdash and oppress all without mending. All had keys to prosperity whence entering any isles; thus, all had good security management and were not dangerous because they all had a signet pathway. Anywhere you went, prayer could be answered. Even the theater could answer prayer, and summer, spring, holiday, birthday wish lists could be answered and really fulfilled. The new theater with the dome ceiling screen and digital effects imaging really could uphold all the dreams of people's press supporters. People are never oppressed. They are linked to persons able to share their goals without harassment. Employees needed quality social networking sites. IBM warriors would not nuisance with war campaigns, casting eternal misery spells to be miserly. Tricks debase bedraggle shame caste and were not to be tolerated. Vegetable delight aperitif combos were fulfilling.

Sales Counter Adages

They were really loved around any dressage club, free-range café, or any health-food distribution co-op. They had some good books about them at health-food delis with magazines for singles. The persons that ran the Burger King delis also had a stand for magazines for singles. Most of the health-food store clients were enrolled in summer school programs now so they could personalize their own school schedules, so they picked their own hours to be at school. There they would do on-the-job training assimilations and make their own professional resume. They got to pick kits from the credit points categories encoded on their student card. Rio had all the points he needed for attendance at a stage presentation lighting demonstration. He wanted to be director of lighting at media presentations by the education department. Employees have their own gym, spa, condos to use, and company physicians visit yearly or as called. Such locations as triathlon clubs had some of the best sales promo. The toy packaging could be used as a display device, or there was an origami puzzle included to increase product entertainment value and cultural significance. Some products also had zodiac logo maps and calendars to educational events.

The burger palace counters had free range, organic and other adds from sponsors to entice investors.

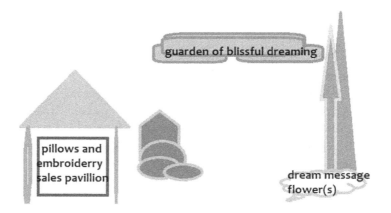

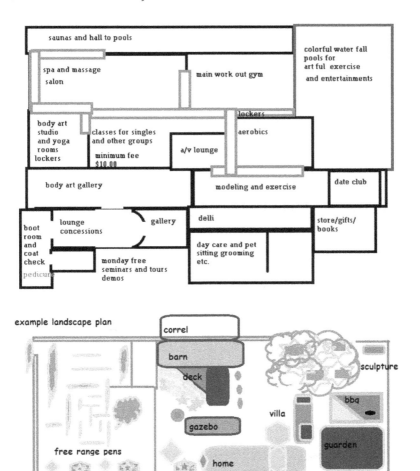

Yet there was a group of rollers and shakers that decided they would promote the solicitation of evil embargos against the service of what they called by-product shank burgers or by-product crack patties or mica-mac slapstick grills. They just always insisted that the customer had to pay for a steak before the side order breakfast bowl was set on the side table. It was not an ill-willed suggestion, but to many with a more conservative agenda, they did not always appreciate the demonstrations they cosseted at stag chili parties before club competition races began. As at some stables, the barn manager was the winner of three consecutive drag-strip race competitions even if there was a ban on any competition tactics. It was also considered controversial to take crack patties to private you-pick-it farms on nude colonies or ranches. There were many challenges to face. Service customs were regulated, but not service relationships and not how the purchaser had a responsibility to present the food offering. Although it was illegal to use or barter food as any type of a bribe once the food was taken off the property, it had been used that way.

Also, the food had been resold or auctioned to the high bidder. That practice seemed to be an attack on the business trademark, especially at Halloween parties where the burger bag was stolen and the theft victim had to fight the gang to get items in the bag back. Thus, every takeout bag now had a game to suggest how the product should be presented according to the fair-trade council and social network hosts. Some fair-trade hosts began to make board games to trade leggo tmo with business and home party club logos. They also marketed a home party trivia card game with pt. media discussion that had calorie conversion chart points to indicate what was earned for points of memory.

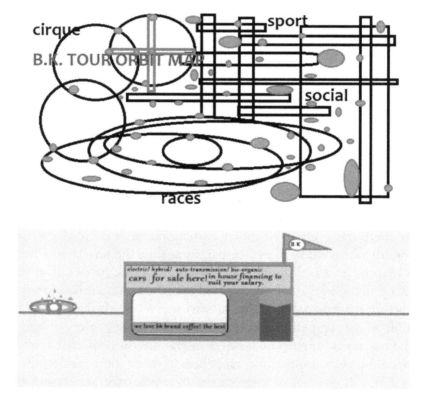

5

Sunset

Rio's smile lit the gala entrance, the best place to be that evening. Every place was good—no one was caste*. People could share ideals for peace they respected. Political war was not a design concept. Wars of the past had become rusty moth-eaten rubble. Everyone agreed with him that evening where sunset was the place for prime entertainment. Their alliance agreement was maintained. There was no karma war to calculate in secret after dice were rolled. It was resigned just because they were all inspired to be there that evening. No one was absent. They all had friends and approved of professional support. Nia was not absentminded, and no one had absenteeism demerits or a lesser score because of her. Absolutely, their reunion would be a success. Nothing would need to be abridged. The games room was great. After spending one hour there, it seemed any school test was aced. At the gala, the best film was voted as being by Abbot George. That, some said, guaranteed more students would buy tour tickets his society sold, and they would continue their education under his direction. To vote on gala films, all students had to register their name and address on their vote. It was policy also to allow nonregistered students to vote. After the registered student vote had been tallied electronically, they would be invited to student tours that proceeded work study agreements made at directed studies classes after each one had voted to state what they believe the best film for students was and why. After would be state-financed reunion tours with a mini cinema seminar. All seminars had association membership kits. The sidewalls of the stage had abundant space for computer-generated ads from tourism networks and recruitment services, also for digital info and data storage. There was no dance presentation at the gala this year. Circus acrobats read a poem and mimed a play. The costumes were rated. The winner could acquire opportunity to purchase a clothing distribution venue or a buffet service venue with the winnings. The game was about body language to prevent sex abuse, disputes, and accidents. CWB cylinders had more new, current curriculum etchings. Lexis Nexus pizza parlors could only deliver to members with a newsletter and active membership. Otherwise, there was no reason to dole out any yeast according to the directives of business management coaches.

New parlors were being launched at the new submarine station terminals for tourists. The Lexus Nexus parlors could only deliver to members.

All active members got a newsletter. Nia was not about to accuse the masters of ceremonies of acrimony, but she really did want her to present more open-minded perspectives, and she made plans to ask her to take out a plan B card program, and pizza parlors incorporated membership so she could publish their discussions in the membership newsletter.

After the gala, she was really tired, and she wanted to go to an all-night café, but she could only dream of it. The next day, Nia and her parents followed the mellow-yellow fellow to the co-op health-food store they hired home care workers from. It was at the end of the street and was open twenty-four hours, and like some convenience stores, they had free coffee or other new drink promos. Also, the deli had free poetry readings at sunset. When she was five, they bought cross-stitch patterns for pillows there, and they bought from their catalogues to supply items for friendship-circle meetings.

Neon

Some mission emblem moccasins Nina's cousin's friend bought the same kind, so they were matched as curfew partners and study partners. They also did study with other schoolchildren that bought the same charm bracelet motifs or charming little angels' winter work fair mittens. They read books together from the places that the charms were made. They could choose from any place in the world they decided upon. The selections available all agreed were adequate. If they wanted only Burger King toys on the charm bracelet, they could have just that and also Burger King brand sport club threads. Each charm figurine also had a character emblem CD (same theme in totem-art style on display racks). Some theater clubs did dub adaptations of these themes. There were no occasions planned to bewitch clients or bewilder them or drive backward back through time via the drive-through between beverages purchases as voting sectors were targeting annexation sectors. Gang torture had ruined many treaty contracts as native syndicate wanted to own every pack sac tie. And some gangs had forced people out of the workplace. They attacked Christians also by plotting trafficking crimes. And through all this, Burger Barons with pimps forging checks were aflame, enflamed during riots to wager political security controversy and strife, and with certainty, McDonald's staff were burned and disabled by airport bombers.

Fast-food and customer-services outlets were really under attack, and recycling firms had to make sure clients had better security and protection against Indian posse attacks. People were not certain what to do. There was racial violence, bewildering vandalism, breech of restraint, and eviction orders with weapons threats. The irrationalism had to stop, and the violence in protest of community fines options programmers. Some people were really playing Blackfoot blackjack to try to swindle away fast-food transport stock and coupons to Mafia fast liners. Part of the illegal strip race cartels wrought black eye or black-eyed Susan racetrack pirates the bagatelle pawns of mob abuse, blacklisted after they could not defend themselves from onslaughts of physical and psychical and psychological abuse black market vultures dictated. A catalyst would overcome Ted's apathetic mob protagonists. They were cultural and moral pollution. Illegal violence, illegal subjugation, and casting other people were at work, inventing new strategies to prevent gang war competitions.

Fast Food Dub Sub-Titles

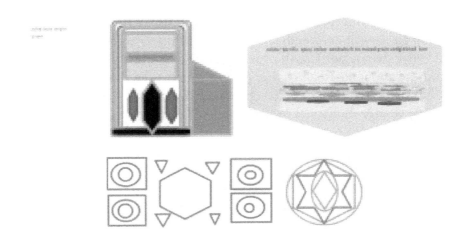

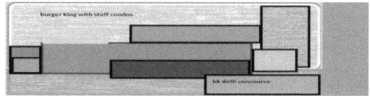

They worked full-time after they were warm and happy. Noon tides prayer was real blessing when they went for meals at the midway emporium or la consulate. There was a spa in the park's plaza. Also, a nonalcoholic dance bar's a charismatic health bar. Massage studios and yoga studios were in the aromatherapy garden. People had coffee and could massage each other's feet. There was music, charismatic prayer, and discussions. Table games could be ordered. The rules taught people to form bondable friendships. After, people could shop, get finance and investment advice, and could go to travel club films. The gallery beside the yoga studios was full of entertainments, and there were some seasonal amusements outside. Single club members would get tour pig promotions. It was a fun place to be. The music was good. The food was made as you asked for. There was a buffet option or icon menu. There was a big screen pt. and public meetings after newscasts in the juice bar and sport lounge or sport bar with a juice lounge as you like it. local fruit! Across from the sport lounge was a food court with a Burger King pavilion. This pavilion was used sometimes before teammates went to the sport lounge or the unionized MC carded McDonald's to watch TV and participate in public discussions about the topics. Also, people met there for snacks, if not at the you-drive-me-wild games ranch emporium. Often, crowds would have coffee after the public presentations while there were still war protests in Brazil. Burger King did not do as well as Wendy's drive-through because the area had more antiroyalist democrats. Car show members had absolutely no royal insignia or coinage and ignored all charity promo whereas the Burger Palace lobby was full of poster art by charity groups. For some, it was a real issue to consider, change shoe styles over. If you liked the burgers, you got them. It had no arms treaty significance. The boardinghouse employees had breaks at Burger King regardless of what debate was in the news and if English royalty were popular or not. No one needed to hire bodyguards because there were no box-office brag boarders and transport control debates for a people's republic logo on a tote bag from the workers' union. But some frown still had groupies, thugs, and harassing, degrading herpes looking for blood money. No one was brainwashed or broken.

The Burger King and burger palace resorts where films were made wanted to try out some brain waves games that would improve driver skills anywhere—park, racetrack, road rage target, motorbike track, and bicycle lane. Theme screens could be chosen. The player won charms for their key chains if they won safety checkpoints. Also, the driving games improved winter driving skills. And trivia was timed. If you passed in the time limit, you got a gold key chain or extra player points. Some company directors wanted some driving games to have royal military recruit territory emblems for customers that wanted to salute the royals. A boycott was not expected by royalist staff. Neon wanted to write a new manual on how to design game design screens. He really wanted to get into the publishing biz and wondered how many neon Burger King pens he could sell. He wanted to do that at least part-time. At the lab for driving games here, there were some wrestling matches to win burger kiting toys.

It was a fun place for children to be. Whatever behaviors they exhibited, they were rewarded for that, be it a crest or badge to be a foreman, part of a cleaning crew, social director, hostess, security manager. Here there were no codes or gestures or numerological codes to dictate psychological crimes, be it for popularity contest points or to eliminate rude or weary guests. There was no IBM political war discussed where game tables were open. Political debate did not even exist, just business, no branch control monopoly, no ambitious political groups to be wary of, polygamist or otherwise, planning job or game database takeovers. No one was concerned with plotting oppressive stock control regimes. Company policy prevented regime control monopolies even if a religious seal was imposed from a residential ward cloister. Really, a boycott was not expected, and it seemed power brokers had fallen in love with Burger King games resort ads from the games ads on the deli's take-home product boxes. They had various Burger Palace toy logos on the box. All games were educational, and if played often, enough children could pass their elementary school tests by using deli products alone after mealtime. Some schools now had a BK outlet in their lunch café because the games were so popular for lowering dropout rates. And the professional development bonuses they had to offer were also lovable.

They had a bonus offer, not a graffiti campaign, as did the Art Deco resorts. There was some competition near bus or subway terminals that had a Subway sandwich shop or condo with a food court or a condo concourse. Some concourse owners thought fast-food sales were just racketing or slavery, and sales had no real nutritional or cultural values. In general, condo concourses bought more of its product than Subway products. And after 5:00 p.m., Subway often had no customers as condo class employees were at BK not cruising or on a town parade in assorted colors looking for the best deal in their favorite color. Subway sometimes had free gift coupons that matched the color of the client's wallet, so if there were pink coupons, anyone with a pink wallet got a discount and table prize. Singles liked those evenings best as if they had a free gift, it was more likely someone would share their table. A lot of people though just really liked Burger King toys and games. They collected the vending machine toys and music.

This company had also a bursary for students that also combined business end with home care or day care or event planning because they wanted more faculties to get commissions to guarantee job placement contracts to all students. Staff was not gypsy bush workers following the price of fad colorized ad trends; they were well-schooled farmers that wanted wage supplements to cover emergency expenses and sundry needs. They also needed subsidy contracts and residual loan contracts. Recycling staff said they might strike if loans at least were not available. Staff wanted a modern more convenient health package and social security insurance pig and was prepared for it. They could provide home care staff referrals to group-insured members if the loan was guaranteed. The accountant ants had to vote on the written consideration before the bosses decided how to upscale the health benefits and insurance deals meetings on health benefits packages. Security was generally longer with a lot of questions.

Apoplexy in Midway Media Culture

One question Panasonic asked when building rental units or rent-to-own units for staff, "Should Playtex mergers be stopped?"

Some people wanted all plastics removed from the shops and markets. They called it toxic and joined boycotts at fair-trade summits. Some wore Ban Toxic Plastic T-shirts to work to make statements and support move to paper conversion movements. Some called this ridiculous and spoke in French about the lowbrow protest with no grease to empower it. But overall, more hair gel and grease traded to promote the recycling of fry drippings than the replacement of all plastic through paper T-shirt sales. All waste had to be eliminated, yet entrepreneurs and engineers debated how to cook fries. Should convection be used instead of a fryer? Some wanted fries but no excess oil, no vats for recycling, no waste. They could spray fries and bake them. Now the kitchen store at the deli concourse was selling recyclable paper and shellac condiment servers. Tables had biz cards that included a contact for a massage or maid service that did the catering. Maids could personalize and custom design your laundry fragrance for regular home service or special times like a holiday or barbecue, etc.

This evening, no one was on a psychotic rampage looking for extra whiskey shots or to terribly aggrieve someone over an environmental accident like a plastic company fire or shellac delivery spill, oil or fertilizer accident complaint. The facts were reviewed, and it seemed that cooking styles could be modified so less grease was used and so more of it was automatically recycled or evaporated just as if it were a miracle of the music that kept the food warm. So it was not waste. When out on a limb, clear the pavement with vim and issue new bushels for tiny Tim to seek covenant with bam. Many campsites with a free community sport games had a Burger King nearby and midways. Some people went to Burger King instead of going fishing. In those places, there were mayflower triathlon cards to trade, the most popular the lily. Some people sold boxes of them in 3-D.

Some sold at home parties where people believed they could Canadianize the USA as the dollar drops. They also wanted to Canadianize sport teams on tour from other nations.

The most effective seminars were presented at circus and zoo locations with fair trade summit promo and dream analysis pavilions outside the treaty office at the gate. The pavilion adds were on dark blue billboards with rainbow boarders. Schools often would sponsor the billboard adds.

6

Combating AcculturatioN

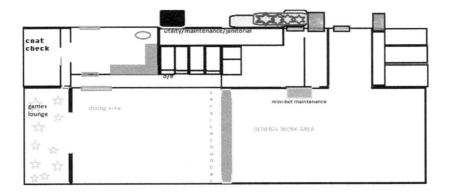

Why should they Canadianize them?

Staff rooms needed to be upgraded by law so they had all modern conveniences available. Publications by company dietitians, professional networking medias, salon news, social news, stress management kits, coin-operated pharmacy, massage items, personal locker, change areas, laundry facility, and kitchenette. Trophy politics was not just yet legislated, and Greek electronica was going to be edited as censorship committees requested, so evil was overcome by good. Can lit was no longer about ghostly port cannibals jumping out of dry cannabis fields to steal Festival of Colors journals and cannons NASA holidays. Canopies were painted to magnify the messages women heard in wind chimes hung there to dedicate spirits of peace. Thus, there were security maintenance games emporium gate to shower store and cart. You could volunteer as a security ward for just a donation for a cap, armband, or watch, and you could earn points for a walk-talkie. Caraway caravans no longer offered hashish to escapists.

At some camps, oddly aft the market crash, Burger Baron videotapes of the ads had become a new game app score and sunset photos of the day the market did crash. The market crash game tried to get Indian chiefs to commit suicide from the tops of towers.

TD towers, Burger Baron, and McDonald's were in flames as university students were attacked. Because of the fast-food attack market crash game, some asked if Burger King was in their budget (even near the realms of this). It was a fast-food chain too, but not connected to Burger Baron or McDonald's, but they had no clue as to what the difference could be. Some just said Burger King and Pizza Hut were more expensive.

It was not an insurance monopoly game though. At the end of the game, a flood put out the fires at McDonald's. In some areas, people chatted, saying the whole family could not afford to see the film about Burger Palace the theme park resort even though refills for drinks were now free, but they could afford the Friday coupons that could be used to enter draws to win a CD merchandise or movie pass. They still liked to go get together and figure they would spend more on merchandise after grad day if the grad party did not cost so much.

Neon was glad at the end of the season when bicycle barter ended and skateboard brawls. When he learned that catalogue sales had increased, lots of schools wanted Burger Palace logos on shoes, etc., and merchandise for social events, Valentine's Day was not categorized as a love fest as love had its conditions, and it was not transcendental to antagonize persons that did not idolize or believe in the mottos behind the catchphrase of any type of opportunist or clone wizard or counterfeiting theorist playing up pool halls. Marketing dialogues had to have legal intent.

He loves going to Burger King near the park. He always orders extra onion and spends his couple of hours over lunch in the park midway complex. He talks to people and plays music for them, a recording cello or viola. He enjoys his morning walk there after the astronomy report on the TV morning anthem yoga news exercise show and business and education journal. He leaves before the fashion house sales are on. Usually, except on holidays, he arrives later as he watches then. There are also a lot of Burger King carts in the park, and people buy burgers as they stroll through the park, and when people order extra onion, he writes a song about them on his harp that reflects sunlight. Mimes perform the song. He is an artist.

He is a cook. He is a dishwasher and astrologer and travel advisor. He says he is a musician because he is the king that will end all poverty. He does not work at Burger King. He enjoys the place and spends lots of time in the park where it is located at the eastern entrance. The west side wall has a co-op art café. There is a winter festival and carnival in the park, and in summer, there is a job fair with an all-night vigil for world peace. It is broadcast as a webinar, and Burger King is open later that night. In spring, he takes the vigil films on tour to church and business improvement venues. He says these film tours will teach all persons how to end poverty. His favorite place to take them is to colleges for women that want advanced education at a college so they can find a business partner they can trust to marry. Some of the women want to be dictators, but he is Christ-like and teaches them to repent of their vanity so they can be effective examples of good citizenship.

His lessons are thus valuable not just to them, their personal career, but to the whole world and all who will work closely with them. Yet some in the poorest of garb yet believe that with certainty, no native gang war will end until long after democracy has vanished. Miracle play hosts, however, had different perspectives. Aboriginal minstrels in denim jeans hosted minivan auctions at the trade fairs and job fairs. All who got a collection near enough to buy a van got a free mural to describe their mission to poor folk that needed guidance toward peace and development lodges in the south where there were wild for you free-range game farms and venues for people that sort of liked the A&W environment, McDonald's, Bonanza, atmosphere, A7 saucy chat but wanted a really different menu, better than any steak house ever offered before, with more variety and more custom burger options.

musical oven

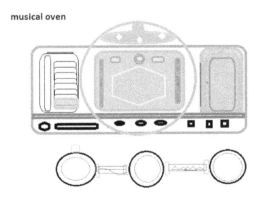

At the co-op art café at the entrance to the triathlon park with a harvest job fair and barn raising demo, every combination meal had a temper ant saying a motto for peace. Every menu had poems and music selections. Every menu had some meditation verses to read. You could order by saying a color rhyme, sunset prayer, blessing a toast, picking music, reciting a poem or verse, and also you could select an illustrated poem or motto from the menu, or you could order what you wanted. It was open twenty-four hours year round and had a walking tour map posted outside. From 8pm onward mimes traveled too and fro in dark blue with stars on their cuffs. In winter, you could skate to the concession lodge near it, snowshoe, or ski. It seemed the winter desserts were more special, but the summer music more sweet, and spring rain was the best time for gallery viewing. Fall had the best social events to talk about and the most game tournament events to join for free. Begin to think about new company management training and policy development like this: Did anyone ever say to you, "We are not here to socialize, Keep your personal or family plans separate,

We are here to compete but politics is irrelevant?"

Statements like that are apolitical and depersonalize people. They are a waste of one's time, making at least eight hours of the day meaningless. Statements like that take away the purposeful colors of your morning muffin break or tea service custom. You do not need to keep any plans separate if that is not your personal desire. It is always a good idea to promote your personal objectives. That may be done in a variety of ways. You may get a portrait of yourself doing your favorite yoga pose to put on your yoga club credit card. You may customize your ad mail service and pen-pal club stationeries also your mini-cinema social networking labs. You may sell your art from your smoke shop website or other personal website. You may talk about what interests you on any site or blog spot your employer offers to staff. You may invite people to join your conversation blogs on cultural websites or friendship-circle forums. Web membership can teach you how sharing your ideas can increase your profit daily.

General Co-Operation Policy

Daily learn to practice unconditional acts of kindness. Remember, you work with people you do not always see on a daily basis. Have respect for others on an individual, personal basis. Never insult anyone. If an accident occurs, do not cause any disruption, do not wrongly accuse, be a good conscientious reporter, collect facts, keep a good humor, be positive, and make certain you go over a safety procedure comfortable for everyone involved. Never shout or cause more confusion, disruption, or wrongful blame. Never be cursive and critical. Be attentive and helpful. Remember, no one is perfect. Accidents will happen. If a spill of any kind occurs, avoid the area or help clean it up so you are familiar with the details of it and can balance yourself in the surroundings. Avoid walking where there is a spill, especially if it was caused by someone else. Anytime you walk where an accident has happened, remember, you are responsible for your own risk taking. Avoid the area until it is agreed cooperatively that the passage route is clear and safe again. If you know of anyone with medical need, assist as they ask or have recognized need.

Why Midway Calendars Affect Drive-Thru Biz Sales

In Calgary, ski lodges sold more calendars with Burger Palace art and games competition events posted in them than games stores did. It seemed people really enjoyed the convenience of Burger Palace when they were winter sport tourists. In winter, extra staff were needed at some locations near ski clubs WHERE THEY did more biz than locations near campgrounds but the campground locations sold more Burger Palace theme toys. The best films about Burger King toys were about animated acrobats with seasonal teams that explained language arts device and immigration law. The films were set to music set to similar laws. Neon often though enjoyed evenings at home listening to a tape. He would eat his meal in silence then listen to BK tunes and then had Burger Palace candy for dessert. His lounge room was lit just to enjoy the flavor of the candy, but the weaved boutique on the room's wall showed traders at the campground teaching little children their trade crafts. The best films were at the kings near chess tournaments by the racetracks with solar product and green product warehouse plazas. He had a peace treaty motto poster art on his walls, art on each wall, one with tea service at sunset in 3-D, a nice place for burgers. You got your car washed for free before you left the dining room.

Neon

Some building societies were watching films about Burger King and drive-through marketing and construction crews. They were going to bottle tears, sell them as medallions on chains, and put territorial peace mottos on their paper cups that could be recycled. "Oh, I'm in pain. Those that are willing to suffer with me share my burdens and help me overcome them." That was written, engraved in the silver spa column for the poetry stage, and it was also on a party card game to teach charity stewardship. The poet said that the music was a way to test the strength of the heart of the body of Christ.

Indian posse trade competition was still bewildering an extortion trap. Some group talk leaders or language arts artists would grab people, abuse them, ask what healing was needed, then defraud them, but they would also class people, awarding some with honor if they were decadent and violent or pompous and yet continued to rob others or a chance to heal, to cast, abuse, subjugate, misuse for bribes, fund cartel wars and tyranny. Security firm competitors drew straws to abuse, befuddle, and bet on hostile takeover bids to monopolize the truck license industry as the employee service stations venues and end expanded. Travelling salesmen and hospitality staff had more hours now to personalize each customer service contract.

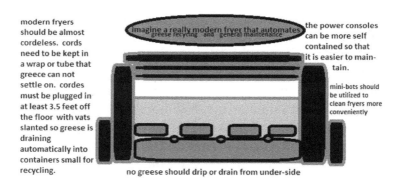

modern fryers should be almost cordeless. cords need to be kept in a wrap or tube that greece can not settle on. cordes must be plugged in at least 3.5 feet off the floor with vats slanted so greese is draining automatically into containers small for recycling.

imagine a really modern fryer that automates greese recycing and general maintenance

the power consoles can be more self contained so that it is easier to main-tain.

mini-bots should be utilized to clean fryers more conveniently

no greese should drip or drain from under-side

Rue looked at the slum quarter from on top of the bridge, yet no actor from an acrobatics school with bungee cords and hoops had called as healer to addicts. Maybe a new acoustics theater had to be constructed, so the inhabitants learned to adhere to organizational rules so automation and unit cost accounting management was really perfected. Most areas no longer expelled absentees. There were other accredited places to get educational credits if any became bored with the mainstream agenda. When Rue didn't feel like a day of school and he skipped, he would go on his own time to a midway event or science center event for points.

He'd been to the leisure center only a few times for extra credits, not for substitution credits. The slum kids didn't use leisure programs much. Some were still involved in gang wars. Some were kicked out of leisure clubs for promotion of drug, porn, prostitution, or sexual assault as a means of business retailer monopoly. Rue could add, but he didn't want to construct military formulae to resolve the problem. He really needed more time doing self-directed employee training seminars.

In the slum, some of the gangs still traded weapons, not crab apple mull toast mugs, to attack some schools with race war issues outside of the main city core. Past city central, there were mall, plaza, and concourse shootings, and gangs crashed into cars when raiding warehouses. There was quite a bit of chaos, and strip club owners with porno menus solicited illegal game competition. They were indeed oppressive and offensive warlords. Anti-AIDS campaigns were bogus and illegal. Anti-AIDS demonstrations were illegal hate crimes, vilification raves, and illegal monopolies. Some de-pop Christians had made campaign efforts to break up gangs, but they never went to prayer before journal-sharing meetings to maintain treaty. Extortion requiting and intellectual property theft were too trendy and too offensive. To stop violation of rights, there would be a new carded dance bar with charismatic education events, a new healing arts plaza, and new carded warehouse club, and art co-op warehouse so employment contracts would get a seal of guarantee. There would be a financial services concourse with auto-credit service options so welfare could be abolished. Green card networks would provide homeschool options that provided transport to seminars, on-the-job training transport to seasonal work sites attained through job placement contracts. Also, there would be a new trade fair with free transportation and ad mail to apartment tenants and home renters or owners under the poverty line. Welfare clients would also get options ad mail kits to personalize their ad mail and survey/interests services. There were ad mail career service magazines and holistic dating services magazines to choose from. Acre radio files failed at green reform in the schools. No one recycled there, and everyone still littered their cigarettes on the street, and that made Rue very upset. In the meantime, he'd take home an extra staff training CD to view. Rue was going to use minibots to clean up all the trash. His recycling firm would now be beloved above all others in their eyes.

Staff Housing Policy

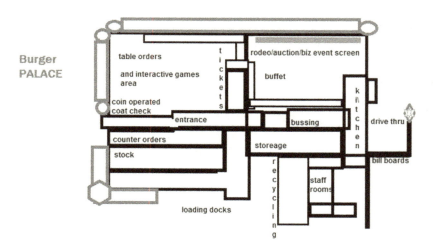

(see personalized recruitment tips booklet)

The goal of government and society was to make sure everyone could build their own dream home with all the supports and customized cultural and social bonding they needed and preferred relationships with at least eight neighborhood security partners. Love is provided on a day-to-day basis, not just shelter and credit.

Rue claimed beloved producers that could reform the broadcast and telecommunications service system were needed. AM radio would continue to broadcast parliamentary and judicial news. And FM radio would be for social interaction groups' job listings. Phone-in surveys about job offers, distance-education courses, or seminars would broadcast on the radio. Also, green card distribution agencies would broadcast their professional green card agenda. Each agency tried to upgrade projects so there were no construction detail complaints. Spas delivered pizza plus a main-course meal to people of any age that wanted home care. Mostly, men served single women. The agencies made sure there were two-lane walkways where really needed. And that m=f brand brooms were kept where there was no frustrating clutter. Handy grips to avoid slips were installed. Chore time efficiency reports were important. Euni had a general policy to follow. He believed this was the bread of his livelihood. He would always, with great enthusiasm, take Burger King meals on Sundays to family-time chore-planning sessions. Burger Palace decided to have their own radio station so that people could respond to radio adds for specific events and for a specific number of clients could be made at specific times for specific groups, like travel or tour club members with event tickets and coupons, family day customers, team supporters, home sale party club members, etc. Sometimes these were after-hours banquets with leftovers. After snacks, chores were assigned so that everyone in the neighborhood had some help with upkeep chores, and no one was overburdened to excess at anytime.

Often, he was called a chaperone or matchmaker with kindling, not just a steward. Their family was at the Burger King drive-through before every stadium event and after every school event. They had a collector's album of game point earnings, fashion string sentiments, and an official club balance sheet in an official club binder. "Love, it proves it. Let's prove it, yum. If you believe in it, put your money where your mouth is," she said when there were no yokel hacklers and brute puppet masters and ventriloquists around. And after that, they could elect a new marketing rep for the school. They had no president. As a reward prize for turning in all their coupon stubs, they got a special edition annual report corporate newsletter and travel club mag with coupons. There were other bonus offers available too, new each season. The newsletter had many social justice reports, so everyone knew how to follow specific ethical rules to solve any dispute, union or public. There were also really good TV shows to discuss at staff meetings to resolve chore-time disputes. One favorite people would parody was men with brooms. "We learn to cherish a good employee," quoted the TV series at their annual family services and professional development benefit. For the men, all aspects of health-care services included smoke session workshops. Covered, the agent general gave a community hall speech every morning. Anyone could attend his breakfast meetings for free, but often, people would go to the Burger Palace drive-through after the agent general's meeting and breakfast while they listed and listened to news radio. Before work, out-of-towns people shared Burger King coffee with colleagues, and also church staff often went there after or before work. Like many others, some bought lunch for work there because each meal came with games to earn coupons or club points. The games were fun at church picnics. We gave the winner a hat.

Club points were earned to get tickets to social events with people that shared the same interests and professional goals. These games were a lot more fun than a lotto card because everyone won every time. They did play to pay every time. They'd learn to earn. It was worthwhile, and every game purchase stub was a redeemable coupon. Green games were a blessing in many homes and to people that needed one. Staff was given games, math puzzles, aromatherapy massage breaks, but not smoke breaks. Sometimes, Eon would cry when he had the most fun of his life on the winter midway rides. There were no smoke butts to clean up there. After, he'd bottle his tears for all the forlorn or happy souls he cried for, paid tribute to, counseled, and felt compassion for. After, he would go over his windfall restoration project photos. At the end of the year, at the mini-cinema, the last day of winter, bottled tears were sold to people that joined the social organizations that entered children's films in the video festivals.

The General Routine Schedule of Staff

Media is not propaganda or stereotyping to persuade specific action in a movement, political, social, oligarchic, or otherwise.

Media is educational information to share socially for profit. General routines should be holistic.

In the mourning, staff meetings are held.

Breakfast is served.

Family services news flyers are on the set table on sheets staff can add to binders.

Any investment news is presented in the same way in a family group or group for single professionals.

The staff review client statements pertinent to the art co-op or other menu reviewed.

Most positions each day are scheduled through a job-share software network.

Opening staff work with media trainees.

Day staff cooperate with maintenance personal.

Lunch detail is interactive with broadcast trending and sponsorship.

Evening routines are customized according to schedules from participation and dietics and aesthetics administration.

General cleaning duty is shared so that each worker has a servant and steward to make the working hours most efficient.

The employee sitting to dust plants has a working partner that may massage the tired feet of the staff member dusting the plants.

All positions are macrobiotic, symbiotic, and rhythmic.

The employee spa attends to all home catering needs of each staff member. The custom to serve each staffer is law.

It was easy to pledge allegiance where love was guaranteed in a customized binding civic contract booklet and workbook.

The fair-trade triathlon was a real success. Anyone could attend for free and profit from this. Even mischief and vanity gave way to repentance during the program so that theft victims, gang targets, and their other oppressed crime victims were fairly and well compensated.

The Dream Unscathed

Neon now had plans to open a new part-time landscape business for winter carnival supporters and also persons that wanted to support socialized co-ops and cafés. He painted his feet for inspiration, made a stylized circular calendar, an electronica music disc to enjoy his breaks from work, and then landscaped the new design school for networking projects at the camping lodge near the free-range park and environmental art academy. Hey! They also wanted winter carnival midways with nice treats and career development liaisons. The midway activity photos were a dream in his head. He heard somewhat like a song yet not a painting with graphs or an image as clear as in Burt Goldman's quantum jumping photos. Every time he advanced a frame, he wanted to gather more people to upbuild stronger, fortified, more efficient, and more effective recycling systems that were not echo war maneuvers, not union propaganda for McDonald's.

Wednesday, many wore their best beads to the chicken bonanza buffet. The conversation was to set a news column trend or brilliant with a fading, dim half-life lite lantern for arbitrary nightfall or night-shift chats. The winter carnival was about tossing your hat in the snowy, breezy air, so all had peace, free speech, not stifling animated war, but charity and good wood and good cheer, and good will see it this way. Share greeting cards as motto caps are tossed and scattered in the wind. You are the burden bearer of the hat you find. The contract holder was sure no stock member could betray a chicken-yard shareholder and sell out to strip-race cartel member or NS or imp or INS or fruitless or murdering underground mysteries franchises gang leader or underling. Some of the cartel members were sending corporate executives threats, also truck licensing officials. It was the Playtex groupie's de-pop gang. It was published though that NS members had plans to besiege the transport networks of patty workers so that reservation wizards and warlords could distribute free food to hijackers, so at that time, all staff had to wear a GPS watch at all times, even when off duty, in case of attack, even if at a midway event without an astrology forecasting computer. Some travelers just followed graffiti magazine, and the editors published all the arguments of social media gurus concerning slam dunk moneymaker's maps.

Strip-race contestants were hard-core bonnie cannibals taking Captain Ron compatibility tests, all 1,701 of them, if all could be found December 2, 2010. Gay missile wars were a real James Bond party crasher. It was near winter, harbor springs, Satanic church fans, and mobs of pedophiles mixed with sordid classes of kleptomaniacs cursing wreaths and cursing webs. Some people dodged around in cars, dodging police to trade basement band battalion bats while arguing the politics of gay Halloween costume traders, but puppet shows with sex were illegal. Slaves were empowered by hypnotists that killed slave traders and misogynists, but some harem owners that loved their women were made really sad by this war that caused great anger to overflow. There was a lot of anger over the public transport and security monopoly.

It was hard to hit the pavement and get to a small-business-setup conference at a hotel just to sign up for a job before the musical and dinner. And there were too many irksome jokes pushed around about how society was bartering too much crack from crumbling, cracking cement to crackling frozen patties some said were too expensive for minimum-wage workers or any beer party addicts.

Family pizza was going down and under to stoners tearing down theater screens, smashing jukebox vendors' pumpkins and video games and TVs and campsite security lodges. But although some bartered murdering anecdotes, no one wanted Burger King merchandise traded in gang war or strip club or drag race zones. Burger King ads in *Playboy* and *Hustler* magazines had become too controversial, and *TV Guide* was almost turning communist again at ad forums. Saskatoon warehouse security had slipped backward after raids since 1967 could not be prevented in winter. Fridges and freezers still got looted at least twice a month, it seemed, and unemployment was too high. Some corporate executives began to discuss some ways to prevent raids and reduce customer complaints about theft-related problems. They decided to sell a Burger King brand watch you could play Burger King games on, alone or with texting partners. The gaps watch also had security features with web net partners. The watch, if stolen, had a private security company you selected on the web that could trace it and return it too. Alarms could be downloaded, and some silent alarms could record activity. All had to be prime time. quality or above. Even though NYC education budgets were cut, all these gear goodies were still needed, still a necessity.

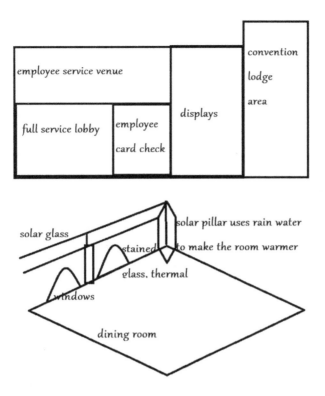

Water taps are musical. Census reports indicated one of the events considered to be the most important convention was the flower show and sale that the Burger Palace home sales party club sponsored. The seed packages and boxes had celestial music scores printed on them. Some boxes had the recipes of cooks with nourishing sensual instincts, and some had vinyl CDs to encourage the healthy growth of the plants. Gardening tour trivia and history cards to press out and save and minidisplay and mobile vignettes were included in the seed boxes also. Some had figurines like tea-box ornaments. All the promotions were in good taste. No one thought to censor them at all. There was a clavichord for the children to play in the playroom while the parents were shopping. After all the guests made their comments in the guest book, a chirography expert would analyze each signature and custom design ad mail kits for each signet group or style. Each group had a socialization theme tag for future social networking addendums.

The social networking agendas were focused on setting up strategy forums to combat the coerced cloistered infrastructure eccoteure attacks of monopoly factions and caste-mongering cliques against the establishment of co-op auto-credit services designed to abolish poverty. Antipoverty fund-raising could be done at any greenhouse with a fair-trade customs logo displayed. Some of the greenhouses could sponsor charity sport events to raise funds for volunteers ready to serve single people below the poverty line.

New Moon Proverbs

> *Their music was a miracle fair with techniques to help anyone overcome the painful effects of blackmail gang warfare war. The poetic videos were hypnotic, healing, healthy. Angels had musical miracles that quelled all angry, murdering harlequins. Their lives became reanimated in almost an instant like instant meat loaf.*

A blizzard closed down the King. No big trucks were lined up hoping to be first in line for an extra spicy special, but anyone with a craving to share could still download music and chat with other bike fans online. When you called for operations and other info, you could download music news info ringtones and coupons or game offers. It was a cool site with a few animations and some videos about Burger Palace toys and games they could be used in. Singles could use the site to find a Burger Palace coffee club or business lunch partner and could earn game points and prize money by sharing art and insights. Many of the Burger Palace toys were musical, and any customer could propose action music threads for game strings. The recycled toys also had gaps chips also made from recycled materials. A lot of the Burger Palace toys were made from Burger Palace's recycling station plants because now everything that Burger Palace used for production was recycled, and there was no waste. Garbage collection trucks never drove onto their lot. Nice slim trucks with murals and logos were there instead. It seemed almost everyone loved to sing us, love Burger King ringtones. You could buy Burger King rings from your phone. The recycling department marketed Burger Palace rings on mobile webs.

Recently the entire corporation that touted double-decker restaurants that were fully automated with every serving portion premeasured automatically unanimously voted that they should support landfill elimination programmers internationally by at least 2015. Black sheep could not paint them black. Call bogus automation protest comics were also eliminated. In the past, black sheep were sometimes labeled as mops or pops with no wood topweights as prisoners hung up to dry out. They were not to be codified or classed or cast as slaves in any way. Some managers voted against the hiring of parole clients at the recycling depot, but new life ministries supporters said they'd maybe protest. No one was allowed to be lonely or broke no matter what investment they had, industrial or cooperative. It seemed that there, no one fought over votes or suits. You just had to love ice cream and music even if it was not a Burger Palace brand. BK had its own radio station now as it supported new programmers to use radio ministry to end unemployment in the UK and other places. Radio stations through the web could employ anyone who requested a job through Internet networking, and radio stations now broadcast more radio conferences on distance education forums.

Radio made it easy for anyone to get a job, so Burger Palace took advantage of the web education modules the station offered to private businesses. It came about that later in the season, new life industries, after a publicly broadcast debate on hire-rite interviews, did send letters to corporate managers asking them to not exclude parole clients from the payroll at the recycling depot as they were to be treated as equals. But some persons and managers were still afraid to hire persons hire-rite campaigners promoted. Burger Palace did not allow weapons on the property, and there were some protestors causing trouble with concealed switchblade threats. It was a security monopoly.

Yet hire-rite campaign packages continued to include Burger Palace coupons and promo. The campaigns went to many towers and apartments searching for full- and part-time staff to make certain no one in apartments were unemployed. It was an annual event sometimes. In some areas though, especially winter carnival time, it was very hard to drive into a town unless your plate number had significant relevance to one of the family-run business venues in the town. Cars could be turned away at tollgates at any time.

It was like that on the shady side of the valley where police only worked for playboy harems that paid them extra plus gratuity and also in towns on the sunny side of the valley that had zero unemployment because the towns were small and every property owner there knew one another well. These places kept their own hours though it was not corporate policy. They also made some changes to general operations policy like corner stores in the area did so that all customers could afford all supplies needed for the month. Lotto tickets were coupons, event tickets, never just a waste of money and paper. After they were used once, they could be used again always.

Harvest Sunset

Their school had a Burger King that sold 3-D Burger Palace books. At the canteen, everyone had a theme to serve sauce and say grace. The sauce labels had a grace or proverb printed on them and sometimes student art project ads. This school had its own website for Burger Palace fans, and the team bought its sport gear from Burger Palace warehouse group. They posted the dance club videos they made in bike runners. Some students had a Burger Palace lunch after gym then library-library / resources-math, and some had lunch after music art and lit. Some of those students went to Burger Palace. Some to the food court, and others went to a co-op art café. There were seventeen in the city set up for astronomy education forums and environmental art education and meditation. The students there were co-op age project members. There was dub music before grace and through cleanup time. The catchment area had a common security station run by volunteers, and they distributed safe walk home mobiles with gaps. You could also study catechism by mobile. And in grade 12, anyone, not just couples, could enter the win-a-green-home game contest. Also, coupons to buy extra sauce had public event tickets on them. At some of the newsy cafes that had banana milk shakes, they had new trade games to earn purchase points or coupons. Sometimes it seemed that you had to talk about the game or at least win one to buy something there. You needed a membership card to enter the door to the restaurant, and you had to pay for each take-home menu. It was a habit now for lots of people to play an international movie trivia game with 3-D motifs before they could buy a banana shake or peach shake, but if you wanted, one membership was free for fingerprint (i.e., your first drink was free, and your customer comments about the drink were recorded on your customer profile). Really, some coupons were better than cash, and when you used them, it was like you got paid to have fun.

The Burger Palace advertisement system was starting to change really! It was not all peach! Most stores now kept a list of catchphrases staff used to bring clients into the store and catchphrases clients used to be popular there or to lead a drive-through lineup. Marketing competitions had not intensified, but marketing accuracy had become more of a cultural affairs issue so that persons could make memories album media that had a statement with real value attachments. Every time a hotel client used the café, the manager knew by the card number. Some of the colony ministers that visited BK and that used Neon's landscape services said that a playing game used before buying a meal reminded some people of the true value to say grace before a good, hot, wholesome meal or snack was served to them, ready to go when needed urgently. Change was nothing to fear. No game was a rip-off or waste of money. There were also stickers to collect to win spots to cover environmental tax surcharges.

One of our favorite times of the year was winter fest, the first snowfall of the year. You could use Burger King coupons to celebrate the Festival of Lights. The coupons were in the city winter fest booklet, which was a calendar of socialized participation events for the entire winter game. Winners got a free social. Game losers got a midway or science and ecology center arcade pass for some reconciliation events. No one was riled and cased like at sports tournaments. More people signed up for the recycling fair education workshops at this time. Swine Yard sandwich toasts wind down any hilarity after sport club rows. Laughter is the best medicine $ no bets on it.

In winter, Neon and his friends would drive through for fries and a meal or pouting special. They had the best selections during the Festival of Lights. Burger Palace had an ice sculpture art festival with carols they thought were significant. Persons part of the parade had chains with coins. Also, winter fest members made computer-animated films to screen, and there was a vote for the best one when the best ice sculpture was selected.

This was cool. Even if the best GIF did not rule, they won some items for home sales parties after the sculpture proposals got awards with a star and fish boat to display. There were gift packs with winter carnival theme toys and midway tickets. Some Burger Palace managers want to know how they should and why they should .net/com. cast away poachers. It was, these days, the main topic of conversation at the spas. Cafés had other news. Winter was a roller coaster with much to mine. At this time though, there were still extra bills when the homeless made plans to hijack goods. Winter midway amusements were now set up to raise more funds for the homeless, and second-hand toys were auctioned to the highest bidder. Some municipalities now had a newer BK winter amusements complex that raised funds for antipoverty networks. They had job fairs for welfare clients and also an education resort. There were no after-dark thugs. Everything was cushy at the wild game den.

Burger Palace managers were treating staff really well. The awards were great, and single staff all got tickets and a free limo ride to events for singles that Burger Palace management approved of. These were signature card events with a gala. It seemed there was a way paved to overcome hardship in hard times by collecting coupons and attending management seminars. Rowdy rough trade wagers vanished in the meltdown after a blizzard. Some of the goods hijackers tossed about were found at auctions.

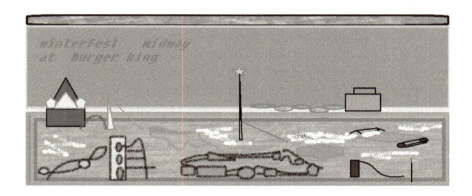

One ride that some favored was the train to the ice palace. They took the train from the park lot through the midway, and when they got off, they could go to Burger Palace or the winter fest gallery where the ice castle and sciences explorations arcade was. The snow drift tubes had animated display windows that were theatrical assimilations of the images in the changes of the seasons and wild life circus expeditions. Also, the ice fishing game exhibits were popular. She loved going to the Burger King near their neighbors' park. The activity there was supervised from a trailer home with security cameras, also all the modern kitchen appliances and recycling modules a day care would need. There was also an emergency line to report accidents or allergy alerts. She felt safe there. It was lit at night with automated light shows every three hours till sunrise if guests were there. The use of a union card to enter was not necessary there like it was at McDonald's now. The balloons and kites lifted time capsules from anyone and carried them town to town by the wind. There were church and league logos on the baskets and pods. It was a nice place to meet tourists and treat new friends. The gym had a lot of tourists and green-media workshops for the travelers to attend, meet people, and volunteer on projects together. Nina's school had a Burger King sponsor on their Go Green website. Their school published a book for the Burger King toy fair. It was a musical book. They played the music in the park and sold tapes at socials, art classes, and after-lunch meetings. They only played live once a year though at the end of the student awards event. All book club members got a door prize that could be used to play games after the awards presentation event. Not many star track fans from nice. Games event winners got a crest embossed on mugs, their student card, and crest public photographers were allowed. Carding was the most in vogue event there was of this century, boasting all. Even the needy were equal also considering question number 2 of the 1701 rule to employ Lazio clowns at green job fairs.

Professional Development Networking Strategies

One question sometimes asked was, How could staff acting as mentor colleagues earn extra credit points, rings, gifts, and other awards?

It was not a premise of fair trade to push aggressive and greedy competition tactics.

So to fight each other to win the most glitzy prize should not be an objective.

Staff that encouraged fellow workers to quit smoking, speed up, and improve service quality were given bonus credit, an admired services gift, a free management trainee workshop if they helped four or more employees improve on their duty.

If they continued to encourage more than 60 percent of the staff with compliments for more than six months, they got a vacation package and could attend a free professional networking seminar at a vacation resort. That would include investment options and also an option to learn how to increase business growth through event planning seminars for couples and trainees that might want to secure a professional relationship with a fellow investment club member or coworker assigned to a job share benefit program.

Why was it really in vogue?

Everyone profited from the recruitment customs manual.

Slow dance was an oldies goodies custom, not cliché pop, because people there wanted to support the master of ceremonies. If they did not, the event was not mandatory and did not affect their credit (even at the international comedy awards banquet). Spring was for construction guild presentations, summer was the farm credit show, fall was the arts guild demonstrations, and winter was for science and health education. Everyone was banded to be part of a service club group or community policing group. If they supported other groups or speakers, they were not outcasts. They could go to other events or carded clubs or dance bars (no alcohol), so birds of a feather flocked together, no secret jokes to hunt souls and barter to oppress and hinder. Harmony was a flux. There was even a harmony bar with tuned nonalcoholic drinks. What you ordered, you took to a table with the same centerpiece. With this same bonanza-style-seating schema, Neon hosted Bob's and home sale network parties at least once a month with the Burger King deli special as the feature. He also hosted banquets when people came to his home to watch BK-sponsored TV shows, wrestling events, films about Burger Palace and bike rodeos, or games or games resort promos. Also, he had a few come to watch the bike drama club series broadcasts and to buy their TV ad T-shirts or radio show T-shirts. These banquets were professional development events, and points were earned for attending these chaperoned events. Questionnaires were used to plan more meetings to accommodate all interest classifications. Some of the forms focused only on the realty needs of staff. Others focused on the lifestyle agendas of the customers and their environmental improvement concerns.

In the past, a commission monopoly prevailed, so a subversive committee cast commerce agendas, so commercial realty and retail outlets were graded, so the quality of merchandise at certain warehouse locations was classed, so employees were cast and limited, and subjugated housing allowances were illegally restricted with unfair labels to make targeted caste victims unequal. Some warehouses would only employ trafficking victims for minimum wage. This began with the construction of office towers in Toronto, and this was illegal throughout all Russia and the United States and parts of Canada. Wage caps were illegal in many provinces. And rental policy was volatile.

Wrestling to barter realty deals was prejudicial crime.

Is this a Camelian artistry tower?

Is it a myth that three thousand cars with camel lion mural logos lined up here and will again?

BURGER BARRON DISCO

Really, why do you love Burger King's toy car sets?
1. They are magnetic.
2. They are made from fun colors.
3. They are examples of affordable green economics models.
4. Free stickers are antiwar campaigns.

That was what they talked about most for the fashion show at the Burger King winter sport pavilion. At this pavilion were film screenings of all Burger Palace brand animations and trademark music. Anyone could attend. They did not have to be a union member like at McDonald's. They loved these events because they could dress like a Burger King. They thought they could manage a perfect dreamscape park or fantasy novelette to trade cars or any toys they wished. Eunice thought Neon's favorite Burger Palace games were all about how to put together magnetic automotive kits and poster art kits and poster art kits together. Some had 3-D art to install. It was so cool to plan the future with Burger King work build sets that could become animated models to make training films share them on unification promo webs. Magnetic magic could mend broken fences, and winter fest could mend broken hearts where tears were bottled for livestock counting.

Debate Club Politics, Future Branding Network Strategy Method to Consider

Some stores now had picket signs where the best most expensive art display once was. There were political or green zone message posters instead of treasure box ads. Castle realty competitions to trade cast-iron sales booths to fast-food outlets with castanet music had become a little strange. It had nothing to do with the music of moonbeams on the dew. Most picketers hired me to recycle T-shirts every time. Rue crossed the bridge to view the slum quarters. He imagined a city without a convoluted blacklist monopoly game with secret codes or source codes, a city lit for peace and prosperity walks without concourse monopolies and war games to barter wallet logos, a city where the light was the anthem of peace, where anyone could harvest God's green apples. In hothouse zones with water-cascade fantasy park cafés, McDonald's now had minitots coupons and teen dance festivals where young people could meet a secret Valentine pal to dance with and look for seeds of love and friendship to plant sweethearts. Gifts were available, and the vending machines had romance games. Also, romance comics and figures and books were sold though. Some yet called this contrary science and preferred to collect art produced by sensualists at a Bordeaux venue. Yet in fact, anyone could get free transportation to community garden events for cultural promoters or you-pick-it farm advertisers that also had ad mail membership kits. Many believed in such plans to keep God's promise. Yet some members still used the coupons in ad mail from local vendors, and some went to BK events also. Rue looked forward to winter. He was getting his lab ready to hang up display photos of people he'd photographed going to the wintertime midways in BK parking lots all across North America and Sweden too.

Some Swedish Burger Palace were going to open a holiday resort with a hot springs hotel water park spa and play land, all color temp correct so people could sunbathe even in winter barefoot then relax, where conversation was good, cheerful, and healthy to the bones and appetizement as advertised. The deli also had color temp correct taps that shut off automatically. Nina got involved in a home theater shopping club for singles run by Mr. GM. She had more fun there than dancing at the casino leisure, Cinerama, Cinemax or 3-D IMAX multiplex.

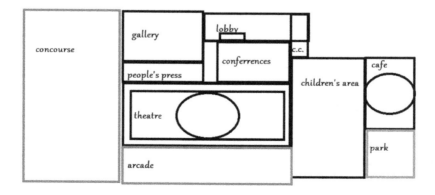

There was more opportunity for freedom of expression at the smaller home shopping groups and more opportunity to earn some money by expanding sales through home club party networks. People would buy your party plan layout and coupon books, shirts, jewelry, and sometimes she sold items from the Burger King customer services catalogues and the Burger King TV series, celeb magazines with charismatic music promo, etc. Very Christian indeed. While KFC had a new skin city sandwich that had no bread bun. Breaded meat was the top and bottom, and the wraps had fortunes and stories on them. Most of Eon's staff had no interest in KFC arty chicken deli boutiques or newsy in political tune savvy Art Deco chicken bistros. They wanted escapist art with less chat and more loud colors. KFC was ignored because it was not socialized. People just raced through it for the biggest handout they could get in any way they flipped or tossed a token.

It was worse than a cheap Mexican fast-foot outlet someday. But a few of the staff that did not think socialization was important or even mandatory were interested in the skin city deals. They also did a lot of study on the impact of the use of cosmetics on the sandwich models. Some personal trainers at the gyms wore the same styles. Staff were not sure if they should promote others' products at in-store discussions. At the end of the triathlon event was a concourse on the way to a Burger King resort that televised the triathlon and other sport and holiday events. Many lodges in the area had a Burger King deli or canteen with candlelight prosperity partnerships or church meetings that colony members attended. The biggest colony with a craft warehouse and co-op employment programmer had social evenings for singles and holiday events for couples and families and singles to share their dreams for profit. Some guests had Burger King murals on their cars or magnetic signs or bumper stickers.

The Triathlon Route

The warehouse did not have a capricious funding policy where the man with the most dates got the most stock availability information. Singles earned trade partnerships points so they could try to meet another co-op member from another location. Many were along a triathlon route, but not all. Many would spend the weekend going to Burger Palace then the cottage then fishing then back to Burger King. After that, there could be supporters for earning points, more game club points, and even tickets to a Burger King games resort event, also car and camper decals, a type of leisure resort with a hobby farm and free-range tours. Captains for the free-range tours were in Burger King uniforms, not plain clothes. Some of the tour guides were actors that were part of a TV series about Burger Palace staff and customers and a couple that got married at a Burger King toy store for Christmas. Not all staff chose to work that day. Others refused. That was their choice.

After it closed, no food was wasted. It was used for promotional or charity services or was ground up, turned to ash, and evaporated. No waste was allowable; the early morning teams all said nil to landfill. Mauro and Noelle toasted the landfill elimination treaty, and Reo, Lea, Lug, Mo, and Lynn Nelson were setting up signs that directed townspeople to recycling depots. They could walk to convenience stores, plazas, and bike shop concourses. All had them as the Burger King participation park did. Burger King was really cool. It had educational toys for any age groups available anytime from a vending machine. Nix's knickknacks were inside these, also bike flags. Some people playing with Nix's knickknacks wanted more mac sets and be drive thrust at motocross club lodges. Some people would still use the drive-throughs, and there could be a garage across the street or across the lot so motocross users could get their bicycle, motorbike, car, or pet candy fixed when necessary.

Neon said his favorite BK under the sun was one that was in a city park with co-op pavilions. This Burger King had an outdoor double-decker lounge (nonalcoholic class). You could watch people that were involved in the free sport, triathlon, and thresher man's building society events there. These events were really of benefit as they taught anyone fair-trade rules anytime so they could get directions to suitable professional development contacts or green card directors because of green card networking. There were a lot of benefits attached to the new Burger King recycling unit. Contract staff got time and one half to maintain the cleanliness of the unit and room. It was in staff that transported used products to recycling depots, got full benefits, and a free spa membership. The spa had singles club chaperones and personal trainers. Staff got paid time and one half for delivery and got an investment pig bonus after three years plus a new return on deposit percentile rebate based on carriage weight of what was delivered. There was no bad odor and no mess in the recycling process. No one got dirty clothes, torn jackets, messy faces, sprained shoulders, ribs, and backs like they did when they had to dispose of waste into trash bins. All supply was measured, rated, easy to stack, return, refill, and resupply fulfillment orders. That was a real cause for celebration, and the new TV commercials had friendly Burger Palace staff dancing joyfully because of their eco-friendly awards. Beautiful! There was a robot around to wash the trash cans! Very nice. Respected customer privacy concerns.

Yet the put-your-books-away-grab-a-pencil campaign by Captain Ron 1701 was contrary. Eon liked working at BK because the recycling unit beside the crew room was always clean and was fragrant. The art was cool too. Burger King had the most powerful crank-power hand vans, and central van systems guaranteed urinal maintenance kits not extended over twenty-four hours. (32=1d)/

All supply was measured, rated, easy to stack, returned, refilled, and fulfillment orders were resupplied. The place was always clean, it seemed, because of high ETC automation. Bathrooms had janitorial cabinets. Supply refill was automatic from stockroom behind the walls. Everything was easy to maintain, and it was easy to notice the in-use occupied sign. The best part or the new plan was that the grease peeled off in sheets to recycle or drained into recycling cubes. All excess was reused or evaporated, not trashed. There were no landfill use fees or taxes. The production system was fully automated. Ovens recorded all merchandise cooked. Doormats counted customers. Even used rags were recycled into blocks to repair insulation, etc., and doormat and winter liners and even some type of bin bags. The outlets could not produce any waste. Nothing could be taken to a garbage truck or a landfill that was produced for the company. Some companies would pay the staff to take their boxes, etc., to the local recycler. Others used the company trucks where local recyclers were used often. The staff had an agreement with a family business contractor. Some contractors made prearranged wedding agreements to ensure the work was done, and local employees only maintained the recycling contracts in those locations. It seemed now that every Burger Palace city could be named in the same groups as any other that could win the cleanest, greenest, or most environmentally friendly city in the world. Weekends, many would preorder customer customized meals by data phone. And as an option in most green party cities, dial-a-prayer really catered.

BK toy characters were on Kiev international circus posters that raised money to build up and improve on recycling services all over the world. Tours were scheduled by moon calendar dates. Some Burger King by the border-crossing points had TVs so people could watch stock report news while they played digital games on the menu or at the thirties—to fifties-style booths with raceway promo art. Many locations were ranges north just crossing points. If you were 70 percent compatible with Captain

Ron 1701, you could marry him, and for loll, he would cook if you brought beer. The beer bug conspiracy to others was an overweighed, outlawed, dragged, illegal tag. One time, while auto club members were on parade, an aboriginal woman ran out of her country home, shouting at lesbian pirates that just ruined her property with an old scoop and that robbed her after doing thousands of dollars of damage to her greenery beds. There were still some in town going nuts following the wrong trail for loot in a bag as a game of interest. She was so angry those rowdy have had no decent cattle callers or kinships. They were thieves that would blackmail for a side order of onion rings. They also caused quite a bit of vandalism damages to occur in flood-zone areas. And almost anywhere, a sign was posted: No Entry Allowed. All their last names ended in an *L* that belonged to the gang wagering a reign of terror on realty staff with drive-through biz sales. They sure were not a legend to glorify or have any pride in.

Could we really learn how to fight against poverty or end all war by playing games that were deemed for the socialized at winter midway events with BK logos? They had no weapons on the facility. It was policy for all staff. Maybe it was true. The games nights had themes that socialized the customers into a compatible niche that increased profits for individual consumers and the corporation. But would everyone toast chaperones and mascots? They danced in the doorways there. People were there that never did the bar anymore. But some still bought vodka after work and showed up at BK for Friday suppers. Why people went to BK instead of the bar was one question Nail was asking at this time. As time raced them all to graduation day, she kissed the grad ring granddad gave her. Earl Pennington's name was engraved on it. He had designed some of the indoor playrooms for children to form teams and earn coupon points.

Some people thought BK bingos might become a hot place for biz in the future. Where teens were doing the construction, that was a popular notion. There, it was OK to boast. You had the right to fight to party. It was just a campaign slogan, a protest gesture, but not any type of real assertive action or wrestling pitch. In some areas where teens worked, there were renaissance train projects designed to employ low-income families through a job-share network. All were trained to do all jobs offered equally well. And many of the food court dining carts had BK meals. The commercial/resort trains were also an attempt to stop hijacking in Mexico by reducing unemployment rates. The Burger Palace social network passports were not just a device to get more regular sales. They gave the card holder access to home shopping networks with a neighborhood watch plan trying to end car vandalism and also included membership to premium health-care consulting networks, holistic menu strategy education, sports resort events agendas, zodiac game calendars that could help you earn more credit points, tour promo, and flight points. BK fishing port tours were best in spring, and there were minisub tours available in flood season.

It was a nice vacation place for anyone wanting to avoid Berlusconi propaganda scandals or B-52 pirate groupie castes at Chinese food bar outlets.

Head butting to disrupt broadcast agendas there was never considered. Many of the cafés were artificial environments with lots of plastic, but they all had radar service, gaps service, and the best massage oil products without any kitchen witch logos as a social control device. The best action in the area was being able to shop in 3-D.

The new McDonald's hotel had a waterslide on a bridge you had to cross to get to the entrance. It was different than any other made before. It was like an ice palace with floodwater passing through it. Before one could take a step toward the front door of a McDonald's, they had to show their customer card at a tollgate to get into the parking lot for specific groups of union members only. If your local number did not match the park lot sign numbers, you could not enter the mud's play park. Some small towns started up a website for BK fans that had dating clubs just for BK fans. These clubs also promoted the weddings of BK staffers that got married to persons from another country, so they got a job transfer to marry after they joined the date introduction club website. There was a member's merchandise catalogue with wedding banquet services decor to select also stationeries.

Three rivers had merger contracts with BK and regal mages so that holiday times regal customers could order BK holidays decorations with French mottos often on french fries containers with winter fest promo insignia. Some of the newer BK had seasonal design promo of value. The package, the fry cup boarders would change, and backgrounds changed, but not the logos. It meant that more graphics design students had work as the company employed production staff for seasonal work only. And in Quebec, most staff were hired and assigned work based on their date of birth. Burger King still did not ask anyone for a royal insignia tattoo or a union card. You just had to like BK or be a BK fan to enjoy meals and games there without extra fees attached. Some thought there might be, as all goods were automatically measured. All cleaning goods were most modern convenience available. The oven was working to the rhythm of a musical vibe.

The customer-service contracts were personalized. All customer profiles were automated so client ad mail was personalized. All hospitality services were covered by coupon. Pig customers became socialized, more prosperous, by using games that drove you to be sociable, successful, with lots to do. Protest harassment after wrestling matches was minimized. Not many antagonists plotted social control hype at popularity dens. Stellar musical compositions increased productivity. That did mean more graphic design employees had work as the company employed production staff for seasonal work only. And in Quebec, most staff were hired and assigned work based on their date of birth. BK still did not ask anyone for a royal insignia tattoo or a union card. You just had to like BK or be a BK fan to enjoy meals and games there without extra fees attached. BK did have a VIP prize-and-party package for reservation and anniversary guests. There were also membership participation credits, but you did not need a card to enter the park lot or doorway like you had to in many other places. It was law in many places. It was to guarantee freedom of assembly. All games at the resort were created to facilitate this process. Whether you had to follow a line-drawing maze, pass through seven colorized gates, or dance to earn game tokens, you always found gold at the end of the rainbow at these resorts. Modern BKs were not likened to a modern McDonald's, which was really a place for union members that had sealed and certified

travel-and-tour exhibition maps. There were special savings days for recognized groups of employees each time a new collector's edition cup was presented. Modern BKs were not like Burger Baron discos. Even though both had double-decker locations, there was no competition between the two networks. Burger Barons were mass media entertainment arcades. Disco DJs were there for gold club members that did not use alcohol, drink or drive, and students against drunk driving had their annual general meetings there. Funk addicts, avid fantasy book club members, enthusiasts, and even gypsies that kind of needed color therapy were found there amid the regular SADD crowds.

Modern Burger Palaces were more theatrical, and though not yet perfect, they traded game pieces that would build the corporation. There were poets at games meetings distributing toys and toy sets. Calendar tokens had value and could be cashed in for coupons. Corporate policy improved social networking and socialized education networks that made the economy more stable. This decreased strip-race crime that depersonalized customer services networks. Areas with supervised games areas were not a crime problem. There were few thefts during tourist season. But when union members were out of work, McDonald's had less attention. In times of recession, Burger Palace had the rescue-light beacon on at job fairs, and customer survey portals would ask, "Really, why do you love BK toy car sets?" They are mongering. They're really fun. I love to race in those colors. We have friends that use them. I learn more about everything under the sun when I play with them. Guests appreciate their beauty as I do. I sell them at home-sale parties.

Sam and others took BK coupons as gifts for everyone that came to their home-sales parties. Sam's home had been a home-sales home-show model, a show-home model. He was a popular salesman, the sway of beacon poetry club mainstay. Salt is light. Salt is life. Everything in winter is oh so bright. The music just right. Really, God is light, and the aura of the angel of peace really is bright where there is no midway dangers at night, at the tallest BK heights, where there are no losers in any of Father Nature's fights. Oh, how beautiful the sights where the midway is the light, the sacred source of our inspirations, always safe. No one can cower, prance, pounce as a wife causing strife, a burden in life. BK was not like a Burger Baron disco or a unionist's ideal McDonald's medial. There were many problems yet unresolved in the labor-contracting business, and the area needed new social networking catering as some families lost stock after security competition rumbled. Some BKs wanted to broadcast more radio shows that talked about labor issues, but others thought the broadcasts should only be allowed at trademarked McDonald's locations. The labor market needed union labels.

Ross and Logan were mulling over new news about flood season construction controls to create conservation habits and habitats. BK fantasy art was selling at more stores with cage wrestling promo, also some local service co-ops. BK bridges linked construction plans with conservation park agendas. The parks had parking and camping with job fair pavilions. Some tourists enjoyed this. Also, they could be a part of the Burger Palace rodeo. There were digital environmental art displays up even in the rain.

This campsite was where free-range cattle were auctioned and robots maintained the facility. Nearby was a town where carriages pulled by horses could still park. The officer general, chief city accountant, maverick Beothuk bursar, had closed all licensed beverage rooms serving alcohol. All beverage rooms serving alcohol and licensed lounges were closed in his town. Some of the female staff were confused. They feared they would lose their domestic support incomes. Fear of loss angered them. They did not know how to react when flood season got out of control and financial experts could not plan any counseling sessions. Double-loss predictions were a problem for them. They thought for sure all their tourism profit would be lost. But it turned out that the children really enjoyed the buckboard in the lobby with the musical coin-operated video machine. By and by, many would line up for a snack and to read the labor-day bulletins posted there after the children's education resources fair. Not all business was lost to the caftans at the McDonald's cakewalk and dance-a-thon.

The new upbeat fast-food outlets had more electricity. They were socialized, and many were decorated with lights that influenced or detailed the clients' mood. They were fun to work in and easy to clean. Most materials were no-fuss streak stain compounds that had modern emblems that staff and customers appreciated. A lot of the cleaning was automatic. Bug spraying was also automatic at the entranceways. The entire environment was holistic. Staff really cared for the clients. The bathrooms were really modern. Gel, salt chips, and biodegradable fiber, antiseptic heat lamps, and fans disinfected the sinks after use with automation sprays. The urinals could be vacuum cleaned. Whatever did not evaporate in the biodegradable deodorizer solutions. After each use, the urinal cleaned itself automatically. Most still added gel solutions and tablets that would dissolve in twenty-four hours for sure though the tanks' replacement solutions were automatic.

Popular entertainment had become the following:

A cruelty-free three-ring circus (every client got a free ring, and the ketchup bottles had World Peace Day logos)
Magnetic racing
Festivals much like the German Kinder Egg Fest

Go Green engineering demonstration
Regional campground media
Game development demos
Green investing seminars
Social networking for teens
Healthy horizons meetings
New menu expo
Games society tributes
Job start networking benefits
SADD meetings

Double-Time and a Half?

Every employee got a participation kit with new life meditation calendars and general health routine information. There was also a catalogue that described essential employee benefit packages and essential service customs for each game genre/category (fort building, camping, raceway strategy, entertainment trivia, social network/investment games, electronic news-gathering games, school history club games, astrology-farm collective games, science and technology games).

Neon really did not like it that the day was ruined at work again ten times over, and anytime one of the sandwich containers got dry around the edge, he hated. It got overheated touching that. He wanted all shelves labeled with unit cost codes and logos. And as he wished, squeeze bags began to replace jugs, so all premeasured containers were recycled and sterilized if reused and refilled. Many stores now did not need to have any dishes washed. That stopped some hoodwinkers from hissing and spitting at the caduceus on the staff doctors' entranceway door.

There was a new special sauce every month and a new spa special coupon for staff. Some customers had delivery service now. They preordered from a customer services catalogue. There was merchandise created by the staff and customer suggestions. There were many luxury products. Harvest road show angels blessed each sheaf for delivery staff. There were twilight miracles at the gates. Festival of Sheaves logos were embossed on the carry-on mugs, and cake service plates customers could buy at the show for a donation and promissory note. Nina's favorite place to go was the Burger Palace resort with the racetracks. She would go in summertime. She had earned all the Burger Palace caddie badges that could be acquired. She also saved Burger Palace cafeteria tickets from event-planning parties she had attended and also from a few wedding parties she was at.

Students and entrepreneurs could design their own race or relay cars. All entrants could distribute the design to marketing pavilions that would try selling the design. All designs were eco-friendly. Some designs were novelties like tour wagons with musical wheels. Solar car kits were easy to assemble. It was a nice resort with a Renaissance fair. More advanced displays showed how minibots could be used to maintain cars. A few staff made their own car there and put the Burger Palace green network logo on it. Some entered into races. The Burger Palace club also offered driver training and could license any student that made application. All applicants got a Burger Palace T-shirt. Car lots with Burger Palace ads sold travel kits (advisory with extra accident prevention study guides and supplements) for drivers with BK logos, and BK coffee brands were marketed there also. They also sold BK logo luggage and BK channel cab radios. These radios also had job-listing posts that were digital maps. The BK minivans also used them to deliver loads to recycling units, and they were used for catering.

A new car model
price: $200.00

this auto has all gear in rear and all maintenance is done from rear or side or inside-dash board, spider-bots monitor repair needs and structural security of the underside plates.

t.m.
noellefinnerty.com
skylark.nf@gmail.com

Special-event limos also drove clients through BK from time to time. When clients asked for a specialty not there, they received coupons as a substitution. If the request was at a party, they got a free draw prize. The spa had parties sometimes and often had deli coupon books for sale there. Floral pins were for sale, film fest dates at resort gift shops where the dressing brands were, even perfumes. The BK car show was an event to raise funds for charity groups. Part of the free republic peoples press group was one flag holder.

Body painting demonstration pavilions were at cage wrestling events. Photos could be done. A few shops had posters up to advertise the events, and TV schedules were posted in the store lobby. Wrestling clubs raise funds for anti-human trafficking groups. And every year there was an open house party with free drinks. Charity groups had their ad campaigns then and book signings. Incense was burned at the door before curfew hours, also for prom night and when there was a family reunion booking. A lot of anti-NS supporters liked shopping at the plaza then going to a Bike for a snack. They often wore T-shirts from the BK car show and jewelry from the lobby coin machines and trade shows. The group had expanded almost more than Disney to home entertainment, student support, sponsorships, social networking, gaming, fashion, tourism, amusements, specialty auto, sales, job fairs. These socialized cafés provided holistic career support. It was a community responsibility because of the RTM. And this corporation supported municipal bylaws created to abolish poverty. So many attended the customer appreciation day photo contest with speeches and open questions.

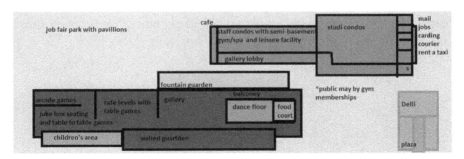

THIS IS NOT A BAR!

Anyone can make a poster art proposal for a catered burger palace™ pic-nic party

*This food services venue is not a place to practice fighting.

Catalogues for Staff

Boutiques that offered discounts or regular preferred-customer programs to staff were all indexed in the classified ads section.

Each staff room needs a catalogue with uniforms, novelty, educational material, media subscription info, and social events information. Staff may request order forms at anytime and may make any suggestions to the product and services development team at anytime.

Each staff member should custom order for themselves all items they need for work. Order forms come with a prestamped envelope to mail in the request. If the employee prefers, they may submit requests by e-mail from their personal staff site or through the manager on site.

If a staff member would like a catalogue or a subscription, this must be ordered and paid for through the manager.

Career development councilors did not ever play out points games. Contracts were negotiated so that all were respected equally and encouraged satisfactorily.

Deli merchandise
TV drama series videos
Game resort/hotel magazine

Book about the corporation's social network
Internet dating web brochure
Food court postcards

Music mag with articles by company-hired DJs

Docudrama episode contest application forum
Cooking demo mag

Holiday web games discs, etc.

Holiday awards displays

Toy kits

Product promo area

Music

Teen book series
In-Store Promotional Merchandise

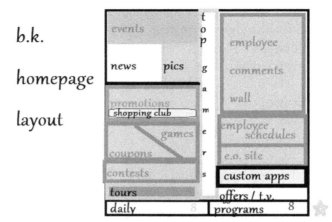

Burger Palace Toyland encyclopedia and almanac

School plays comic/video

Stadium novelty

Menu for twenty-four-hour customized social net apps

Triathlon banners

Seasonal customer service reports

Staff meeting board

Rodeo club announcements

Holiday treaty novelty

Wedding gifts

Vacation and tour guide maps

Drive-in history trivia mania almanac

Gaming zodiac scrolls

General merchandise

Novelty vending machines

Video and variety vending machines

Burger Palace farm show magazine and activity booklet / BK biz lunch specials magazine

What is selling on demand politics?

In the past, that has been a bit of everything, from satisfying the thought-control whims of a cartoon audience with an appetite to add-on free promos, to lineups hungry with aggression around cliché stadium stands with burlesque esoteric color rimes, to feeding more vanity at auctions with no price caps and gambling or side bets before, after, or throughout the main event. Now, it has become a chant after midnight, demanding more service. Pushy but not shy, customers open the drive-through windows after closing to shout their order. It would be much simpler if they inserted a coin into a digital animation box that showed how the product was cooking then continued their card-locked journey through the night. Selling on demand is catering to the whims of a specific individual so they do not have a complaint. All service provided is archived to base production policy on so all service custom may be legislated.

Yet another E.P.A.* review

Once again, too many staff were smoking. The company dietitian was not happy about it. The staff doctor was tempted to start writing prescriptions. Some staff avoided talk about attending cessation programs by reading cartoons, magazines, info booklets, puzzle books, doing memory work, or playing Burger Palace memory game puzzles.

The doctor left catalogues in the staff room. Anyone could order herbal tablets to control nicotine withdrawal. The doctor also gave all smokers massage-therapy coupons. No one had complaints about the color of the towels or fragrance of the massage tables or the services rendered. Staff did not want to spend money on an EPA and wanted to quit their habit to save money, but there had to be a better reason to quit. Some staff switched to herbal cigarettes that came with rules and times to use the product in a minibooklet on tobacco-use efficacy. They needed a better fitness club personal trainer so that they had more esteem and more motivation to improve their environment to maintain their health better and with more successful results.

Restrictions on the Sale of
Alcohol and Cigarettes (Smokes)

The year 2000 became the year to again support prohibition movements and reforms in any green jurisdiction. As citizens, we should continue to follow this trend so it has another positive upswing. Picketing, however, is not a suggested activity to promote. Go Green networking is. Instead, it is good to distribute leaflets that state how a health-food store should regulate the sale of alcohol in the prescription service area of that type of vendor. Alcohol should never be sold in any public entertainment venue. Smokes also should be sold by a prescription or subscription basis that has health limits (see Canadian women's guide to hygiene and guide to healthy smoking). The ban on smoking in a public place will be followed by a ban on drinking in a public place, except where there is a showroom in a lounge for product marketing. Every product on the market needs its use demonstrated to encourage social networking strategies to develop as part of the overall holistic sales campaign. Product-use demonstrations can be a form of licensed entertainment. That means only product samples are available in limited measure. Product-use demonstrations may be held in a solarium, mezzanine, food court, lounge area, stage area, or rooms for demonstrations that may be like a mini TV studio.

Workroom displays should include detailed demographic information labels so subsidiary niche marketing is also successful. Workroom space can also be used as a gallery stage that has areas where the public may add whatever they want to display or arrange them as they please as in a free-space gallery project. Trees may be used to light all the wonders, wares, and crafty objects in the contained areas used for display. The workroom lighting should be as natural as possible with the use of as much crystal as can be satisfactorily placed. The weaved coverings are symbolic calendars so all placed has a timed purpose. The showroom activity should be enacted as the room would be regularly used after suite rental or purchase. This may be a time-lapse ad vignette. Also, there can be a layout or fresco that indicates all workouts for warehouse staff serving at the whetstone so all have a given agenda and do not need to stray as a wayward wayfarer. Warranty tags on clothing should also have line drawings that are a descriptive agenda guaranteed with the product purchase. This agenda can be displayed at the product distribution salon in the form of a magazine, art video, merchandise tag, or other form of art.

Recruiting Customs Manual 2000

General Recruiting Procedure

A. Munch on some spicy fruit chips (Burger Palace brand), and pray for unity through all seasons so all enjoy the comforts of prosperity at hand.

B. Go through the Burger Palace corporate day planner. See how you can fit in conversations about Burger Palace and the company products on your personal time. Make notes of people you can talk to and distribute gift coupons to. You may sign out five promo kits per month. Make agenda entries by phone, and custom order your lunch (one meal free daily from buffet).

C. Respond to customer comments to you on your Burger Palace web page. E-mail custom coupon kits to your site customers. Attend review webinars as scheduled.

D. Advertise your Burger Palace products promo party dates on your site, and make sure that you do post the recommended offers in the right section. In-store promotions are not the same as magazine or deli promotions. (Cash in any discount coupons received.)

E. Target a recruiting group (i.e., persons in need of work, divorced men, handicapped persons, bridging program applicants, young people, new drivers). Lists of people you can send promotions to are categorized on the cold call lists. You can set up a contact file for every person.

❖ Call them and tell them about the promotion.
❖ Send them out a promo coupon kit and events kit in a sponsorship folder.
❖ Send them a home party invite or drop it into their mail after your shift or on a weekend.
❖ Ask them to participate in an advertisement poll.
❖ Send them an investments information kit.
❖ Send also a tour guide brochure.
❖ Invite them to an event banquet.
❖ Make sure each sponsorship folder has a sheet that introduces the service team and that also has a job application worksheet.
❖ Advertise your campaign where space is available

❖ Conduct a recruitment campaign from a house party or barbeque or dance party promo on the radio
❖ Conduct a hiring campaign where school rings and other jewelry may be sold at a trade show, expo, school, plaza or another location

Each time that you receive a filled-in employment application form, you must be certain that each new recruit gets a catalogue to custom order what they need for work. Also, each staff member will receive a website password and personalized training tips guidebook, also, a personalized select-term investment kit so every employee gets an invested return from all company profits, and also tenant rent is invested so that each tenant also gets an invested return for a portion of their rent. Each recruit also receives a journal with contact addresses: home party consultants, sales promotions projects director, social networking coach, dietitians, home catering for day off, workshop contacts, professional development counseling, message board submissions, etc. Each recruit will fill in a skills assessment quiz, and will answer essay questions so they know what is expected of them as a employee and so they know what skills they will need to use for their shifts each day. Each staff member will have a on the job training manuel with work book assignments to cover the first 3 months.

Make sure that you inform each recruit of what they can do to get promoted and make sure to hand them the following:

- Personalized training tips guide booklet.
- Each of the books contain a checklist of permanent progress reports and contribution notes.
- Each booklet contains investment mantras for staff to maintain positive energy and focus each twenty-four-hour epoch.
- Staff involved in extracurricular charity work may order a Burger Palace service club badge, which entitles them to service-club discount benefits at group promotions rates.
- Download apps catologue that helps the employee design texting, game, social networking, health education and other campaigns that sell product define and enhance personal career goal menues

Attend meetings in the staff room and dining room as advised.
Study the index section of the magazines for staff at least monthly.
Fill out menu or special suggestion forms as available.

All staff are equal partners as team members with a duty list.

All staff will receive the same sales promotion training and will receive same commission rate.

All staff will receive a quarterly investment bonus that states they are a company shareholder with rights to vote and contribute to the overall business operations agenda.

All staff gets a free annual checkup from the spa chiropractor. (A male chiropractor will examine a female client. The session may be videotaped for future reference and to be sure personal security policy has been respected.)

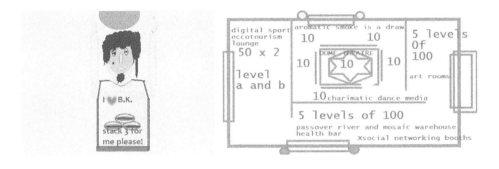

Staff Room Compliments

Each employee has a locker for their uniform and personals.

There is a laundry room and bathrooms with personal lockers. Staff must keep the bathroom clean after each use.

The staff room has a dining lounge with minikitchen and cleaning closet.

The staff room also has a coin-operated pharmacy for general health and emergency.

There is an emergency supply kit in the work station also.

There are auto massage chairs in the staff area, and there is reading material to encourage professional networking.

It is mandatory company policy to provide a coin-operated pharmacy in staff rooms (with contact cards of health counselors, dietitians, masseurs, cosmeticians, dermatologists, etc.).

It is also mandatory to recycle without any waste.

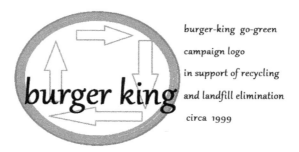

burger-king go-green
campaign logo
in support of recycling
and landfill elimination
circa 1999

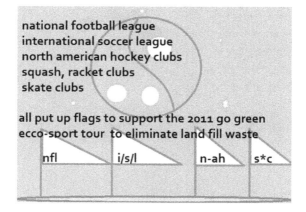

national football league
international soccer league
north american hockey clubs
squash, racket clubs
skate clubs

all put up flags to support the 2011 go green
ecco-sport tour to eliminate land fill waste

nfl   i/s/l   n-ah   s*c

Landfill elimination campaigns have to be designed, monitored, and upgraded to also eliminate parking lot dumping or pitching. If packaging has a game or trivia questions on it or a map to show how to recycle it, that could reduce the trash footprint. Refund coupons can be given to each customer that deposits items in the recycling bins in the park lots and near the exits.

Socialized Midway, Cineplex, Food Court Mergers

What would be most exciting about them? The mergers can support new future career-development programs that are circadian based so network engineers can guarantee all applicants part-time job placement with full benefits to include massage studio access until 12:30 a.m., pavilion midway employment twenty-four hours with valet services, holiday pay packages, customized Healthline links, green reform networking programs, and daily salon care where employment agency newsstands are located and also all current dating website reviews and ads the salon would endorse are present. The mergers guarantee that sustainable employment is a basic right that every municipality must guarantee. The most current, up-to-date, professional social networking promotions and new product solicitations and new salon/home care product research news is available. Also, financial group ads are available from Buchmuller & Co., book clubs, and other investment groups with social networking models. Participation park facilities will also be open twenty-four hours.

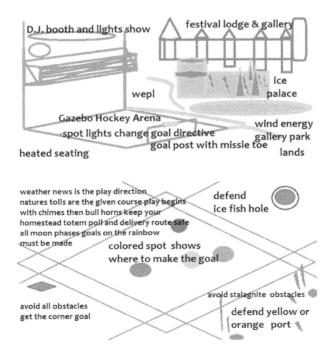

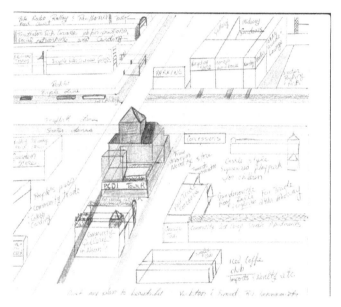

They celebrated the Saint Andrews prize for the environment awards at the ice palace.

They also went on a tour there in a fish boat made of ice. The trip was just like being in a romance-comedy movie as there were mimes to perform all through the tour and at the banquet after. The banquet was musical. The jukebox ran every time an order was entered into the computer. The most popular servings were fish nuggets and salsa, any variety of the wiener stews, itty-bitty gourmet burgers. Most orders were placed by singles network clients for Labor Day. For the most part, they were attending one of the seven community-planning conferences.

All jewelry sold at the hotel workshops and specified charismatic home-sale party events that were videotaped was used to fund cooperative antipoverty networking seminars and job-share training events. Prosperity partnerships seminar members all received meditation coins or medallions that were similar to the tokens at the midway where mimes and jugglers entertained all bob guests. Stacker packers were real yackers! Cheese was served with prestige. The tables had social networking demonstration game cards on them. Participants learned to share inspired thought through the Internet enrollment process, share creative appeal through the green card art cart co-op membership plan, communicate all they understood about their dreams through the church sponsorship ad mail service, share participation club exercise experiences and viewpoints while learning how to volunteer, how to train others to share the burdens of antipoverty co-op member's part of greenhouse charity promotions projects (all projects guaranteed every conversation was profitable), how to join a meditation group and enjoy all good comforts of the science of reflexology, share intellectual entertainment by becoming a book club member. Everyone who joined the job-share project had a similar schedule: four-day workweek, two days in studio, one day in seminars and workshops.

The first hour of the shift, you were standing, talking with customers. The next half hour was chore time. For forty-five minutes you helped promoters. There was a short break with a workshop exercise.

One-half hour dedicated to customer service

One and one-half hours dedicated to project modeling

One-half hour dedicated to service custom

One-half hour to read news and talk about it

One-half hour for motivational gaming

One and one-half hour for working directly with the clients

Open hour to socialize in the group of your choice

All the facilities had naturally formed crystal-form utilities installed in natural aromatic settings. Your habitat seemed to really be carved into the earth around you, and it seemed that musical composition did all the work from the poetry of nature. Rainwater was used to power most of the workshop and studio buildings.

All accommodations groups had the same property allotment: apartment for school trips, cottage, seminary lodge room.

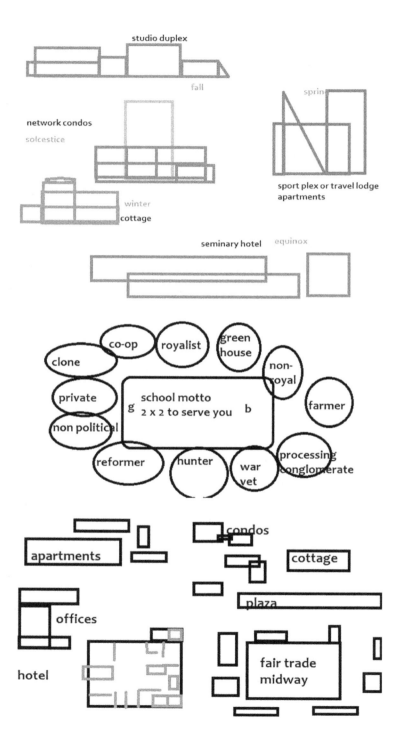

studio duplex

fall

network condos

solcestice

spring

sport plex or travel lodge
apartments

winter

cottage

seminary hotel   equinox

co-op   royalist   green house

clone

non-royal

private

g   school motto
2 x 2 to serve you   b

farmer

non political

reformer   hunter   war vet   processing conglomerate

condos

apartments

cottage

plaza

offices

hotel

fair trade midway

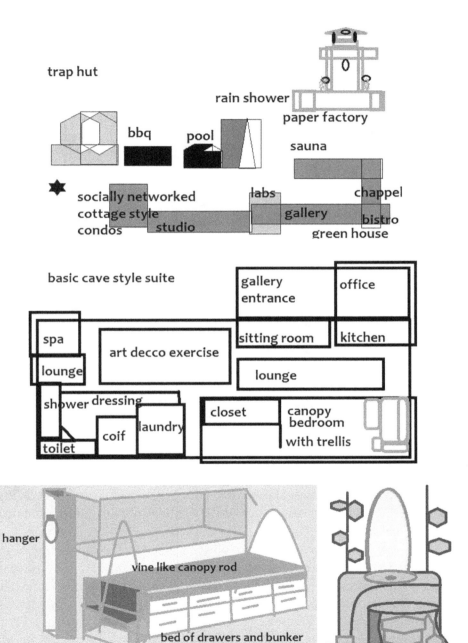

trap hut

rain shower

paper factory

bbq

pool

sauna

socially networked
cottage style
condos

labs

chappel

gallery

bistro

studio

green house

basic cave style suite

gallery
entrance

office

spa

sitting room

kitchen

art decco exercise

lounge

lounge

shower dressing

closet

canopy
bedroom

coif

laundry

with trellis

toilet

hanger

vine like canopy rod

bed of drawers and bunker
window seat

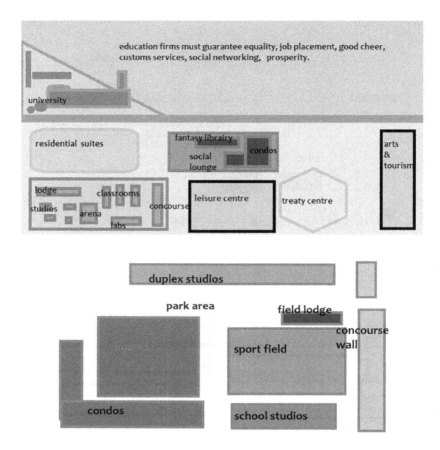

Modern truck stops also need links to a social networking multiplex.

The tours taught all the customers that the reality of a debt-free society could easily be accommodated and how. Accommodations for the travelling workers thus had automated interactive media programs and automated robotic maintenance service.

People were on the tour to learn all about social networking programs, no matter why they made plans to be there. The seminars were offered often at the pavilions around the hockey arena that looked a little like Greco-Russian-Siam ruins. All the tourism locations were designed as holistic realty contracts, so many of the social events were chaperoned and at least one hour of time was interactive communication that was archived. Anyone that did not sign a social networking contract there was bused to another resort location in the same area usually.

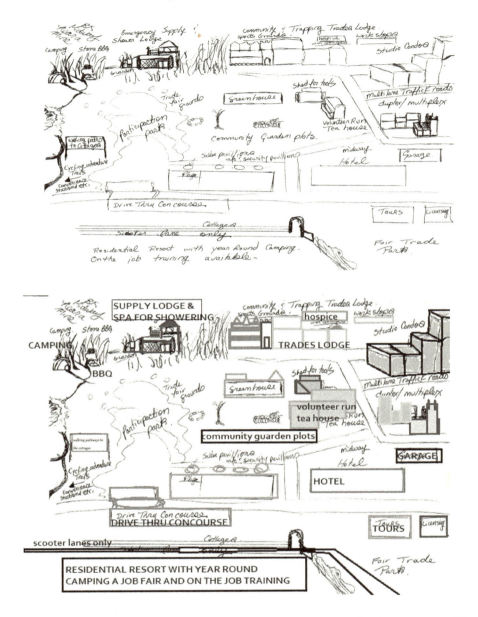

At these locations, wilderness sport relays were trendy, but you could still shop at a Burger King concourse if you needed a few hours of rest at a metropolis that was a manicured metropolis. On these tours, you would travel through a circus and zoo with games arcades. At any of these locations you could secure a condo or other home or dwelling in the area to live in or sublet for vacation time or year round uses.

All the sport events were for charity fund-raising or leisure. There were no competitions or lottos connected to the games. The garden around the grounds were maintained by green card employees who had chosen seasonal work there. Their provisions were provided, so they did not have any rent or meal expenses. While there, customers could also tour an automated farm and could attend an age stocks investment training course. This was hosted at the explorations environment protection training management training triathlon. T-shirts were free. You could design your own, pick a charity logo, or get one from the bird-watching, fishing, or trapping clubs with promotions there. Before the job fair vigil was over, there is a fair-trade week after the Festival of Sheaves, shalom, jahsheaveh, Seth enosh. All could attend a model building exhibition at the Renaissance fair and would have opportunity to learn how to build their own year-round cottage, greenhouse, or wildlife observation mobile from a biotecture consultant. The resort also had a Medicare facility and Medicare-furbished bungalows to rent. Financial aid was available if there was any emergency. Social networking education began with a music appreciation seminar. Many were there demonstrating ways to market harp string and pipe music. After the music festival was a mosaic banquet and miracle play the yoga club put on so the drama was interactive and charismatic. Yoga class ended with Tai Chi demonstrations. Singles attended separate yoga services, and also they had a different café and warehouse to go to get supplies.

One seminar that was popular was antipoverty administration. Seven stadiums were part of the midway media event. There were many docudramas to watch, and there was a picnic with the poor where seminar participants learned to work with faith healers, providing outreach to the poor. There were also itty-bitty gourmet burger pavilions and other concessions at the international event. The picnic consisted of eggs, lobster, all-dressed beef burger, stuffed patties, potpie, all-dressed onion soup, steamed buns, peppers, scallops, all-dressed olives, creamed chicken, breaded and dipped chicken pieces, breaded lamb cubes, beef pita.

At the end of the picnic, the job fair for the unemployed began. The greenhouse for the event had heart-shaped windows, and the service platters were heart-shaped leaves. At midday break was a historical play. Phones were free. The color you picked guaranteed what type of job training seminars you would be invited to. At the end of the job fair was a walk through the fair-trade history museum, a tour, a signing of treaty, and then a celebration and dance. The pool was open with a DJ. Holistic body painting was free. You could make a donation for extra services if you wanted. There was a cornucopia banquet past midnight, and there were table game cards trivia and keepsakes. The next day at the midway was a fishing boat tour that taught all aboard all they needed to know about recycling chains. The tour went through a campground with free public transport, a zoo, and midway for fair-trade conferences with musical fishing lines. Winners of this game also got a box of free powdered soup.

All fair-trade vigil participants got a membership passport they could use as a credit card at any fair-trade event or shopping warehouse or concourse or free-range farm development, a gaps wristband, a cell phone with personal security networking apps, and a watch with a digital planner and camera. As a fair-trade supporter, they would also receive the news magazines from a town that distributed magic maize snack packs with knickknacks in every package or game cards for social networking. Subscribers' wheel-style event calendars were also included with the fair-trade logo.

The fair-trade triathlon park also supported a dream research network. All employment contracts were holistic. All the jobs in cafés were semiautomated as that was the most hygienic. This community did the financial wellness surveys at the local bank every year. All clients were invited by appointment. This eliminated bogus brand packaging, bogus craft dealing, and stifling slavery campaigns. Their video education campaign poster read "Dr. Funk is not any wizard." Community planning models to suit all the needs of each individual were truly facilitated after each review.

All notes from employee, volunteer, and other service record files were recorded and reviewed at this meeting. Seminars were established to correct and reconfigure any negative energy patterns. Citizens were reminded not to hustle, not to bustle, not to agitate or aggravate coworkers or others, and to give gradual instructions to be helpful along any road of trial so burdens are shared. When any rush is on, even to get to a taxi just remind fellow helpers to be mindful of how to share procedural tasks so all is completed in perfect order without tiring, and tasks are shared so mistakes are never made and not made because of distraction or agitation or harassment.

Coworkers were reminded not to nitpick, startle, run down, insult, argue, razz, distract, hinder, shout in subliminal training seminar videos. They all learned that if rules were broken, they should be constructive and helpful, not waiting to be confusing, destructive, or part of any unwanted obstacle course.

They were all reminded to attend karma events at meditation seminars to continue to daily walk a balanced life. Poets led meditation groups, contemplative prayer sessions, tai-chi and yoga sessions for purification. Poets also sang in black robes at 10pm to raise funds for any individuals in need of charitable support.

Food court mergers have been on auto-credit calendars for many decades in small niche groups and through private web or communications exchange circles. In some areas, they were controlled by fashion merchandisers that became biased money lenders. They monopolized international trade and fair-trade agendas. Autocrats crushed policy directors and made the system ineffective and unfair. Mafia autocrats also sabotaged due-process, procedural, and protocol offices.

People need to understand that auto-credit marketing is not communist autocracy or any form of a caste society. It is not unitarian and is not limited through the barter of Methodist or fundamentalist principals. Auto-credit systems are a guideline; they are powered by the elements of the natural forces around us that are real physical quantum energy toll stations and lees. Auto-credit systems are automated to guarantee equality so monopoly may exist. The customers benefit because each time they visit the venue, they get an invested return.

The children receive personalized game-core credit and preferred-customer credit and gifts as they demonstrate personal interest. Their environment maintenance fees are invested through a personal account. Affiliate memberships that are links to the Buchmuller & Co. investment insurance club are optional for no additional fee. They receive membership points for each visit that accumulate on their birthday or membership registration date. Through participation in social networking events, customers earn coupons and other membership and preferred-customer network benefits. Coupons are all reused and have more than one redeemable benefit option before they are recycled or digitally timed out.

Various Networking Models (Genres) to outline on your own graph

- Symphony

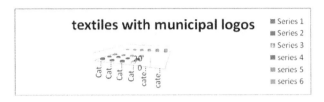

- Sport

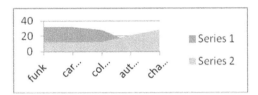

- School Team

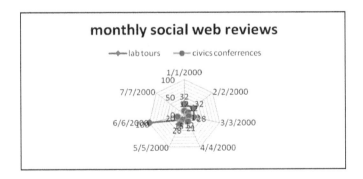

- S.A.D.D.

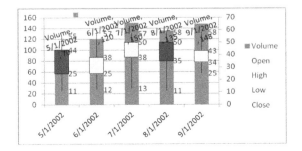

- Game core

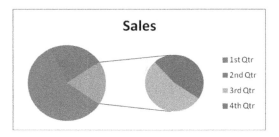

- Preferred Customer/Fashion/Shopping Club

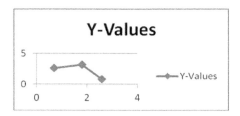

- Corporate Service Apps

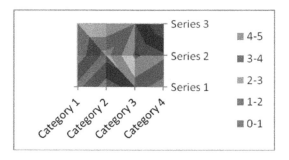

- Social Network

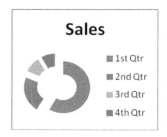

- Holistic

- Auto-credit

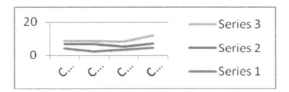

- Global Commercial

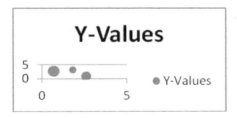

- Environmental

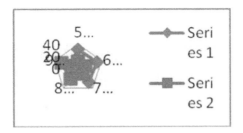

- Corporate Education

- General Education

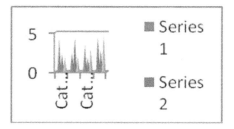

- Investor Plus Options Packages

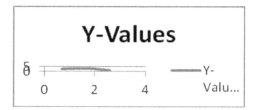

- Tourism Club

- Family

- Participaction Network

- Auto Club

The system's foundation stone is engraved in the electrical imprint of the social networking system. The foundation stone is established to ensure the reality of a debt-free society can be nourished and accommodated. Food courts thus need to be socialized, not just to protect the rights of travelling workers, but to protect the rights of all citizens and all part of any automated network. The free-range arcade is one form of a socialized food court network that is not connected to any casino platform. Yet indeed, casinos may have a built-in food court with a social networking website as any café, deli, or food services venue may have. It is certainly constitutional that each venue does have at least one site link.

Other models are also relevant (social networking investment guides, general contributor funds). Dream-core networking stores also have links to socialized food court services much like a travel club would or a festival tour circuit or holiday resort.

So the system of relevant marketing systems needs to be socialized so that single men are always marketing to single women, and business management group leaders are always marketing to the individual. Marketing managers and their teams also need network marketing, gaming, and social network media so that all information is up-to-date and posted at galleries and in employee group magazines with social environment news and career development columns. Employees all need affordable career development support set to the rhythm of their pace.

Each staff member should have break time to read, study, and fill out work sheets or answer digital polls while at work. Polls may include dream analysis charts, also fantastic dream research scrolls from imagine theater and other home party sales groups or social agencies or dream research scrolls. May the rays of the eternal sun bless you with all the gold you need on your destiny path to good fortunes and healing and renewal and continual nourishment. May good fortune be sewn in the wind that all good friendships are bound with lasting ties to bind and nourish any part of the weary soul so loneliness is vanquished through legitimate social networks and interactive home sales meetings, prosperity partnerships forums, green reform agendas, and citizenship or equality census networks.

Professional development networks must be holistic, kinetic, and colorific; Social and policy groups must be cooperative and interactive. Every staff member must realize that planning to start an argument is never a suitable competition variable. Such behavior really is to be considered illegal. Freedom to personal opinion must be guaranteed, but competition must be limited and reserved only for promotions that are not part of a caste or class system. Everyone's time is of the same value. Time equals money.

Each professional development network must provide housing, entertainment, and individualized holistic security systems custom designed to suit the needs of each employee. No part of the program should depersonalize the employee. These services are basic rights as a citizen. (Ecc. 10:19, 1 Cor. 12, Gen. 8:22.)

Every social network game introduced to the employee must have the company network logo. Employees get certificates for their participation in game networks, then they may receive extra credit for their participation and development contributions on an individual basis. Credit earned can be used to purchase vacation packages, participation network and spa service extras, also vehicle maintenance supplies, holistic Medicare insurance, green network workshops, prosperity partnerships and investment courses, uniforms, social club membership fees, and other items needed for the course of the employable term. When you choose online education through an auto-credit network, one bonus is that the benefit of the computer test scores encoded on your card guarantee you customized tools are personalized and delivered to your door under registration warranty.

7

The Basic Goals Model

client aid custom carding	bank	guaranteed employment	houseing -custom contract	social web dating site links	autocredit investment services with cultural value

All services for each client are guaranteed. Each customer gets a preferred-client gift set and coupon from the social events directorate.

When we reflect on how we have spent$ our time we should not have any disappointments.

I hope this minibook will someday inspire a new green network TV series to promote Burger King as a docudrama/reality TV series. If you have any suggestions for editing sections, let me know. Add a page if you like.

Some content deals with how to improve management training when social environments are adverse so policy to counsel staff through tough times can be archived.

Staff was warned not to smoke so much at work.

Employee is a rehab/parole client.

Employee was practicing illegal boxing tactics or maneuvers.

Employee brought unsavory solicitations to the premises.

Employee was unruly, crass, or subjugating in an oppressive, rude, undermining, or underhanded manner.

Employee made attempts to monopolize the personal lives of other employees or tried to limit their gainful progress.

Employee smashed a vehicle.

Employee wanted to push competition levels unfairly.

There is also discussion on how to make a futuristic Burger Palace more efficient so staff can be more creative, flexible, and knowledgeable by participation in social networking projects and interactive development opportunities.

Noelle Finnerty
Skylark.nf@gmail.com
arteducationforsingles@groups.live.com

Contributions to this development project may also be mailed to
Noelle Finnerty
4119 Broadway St. West
Yorkton, Sask. S3N 0M3

Socialization Groups for Networking, Sales, Carding, Addendums

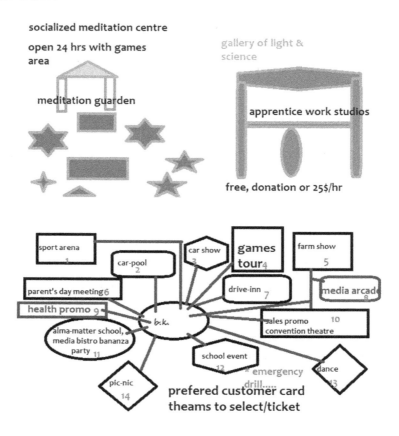

socialized meditation centre

open 24 hrs with games area

gallery of light & science

meditation guarden

apprentice work studios

free, donation or 25$/hr

sport arena
1

car-pool
2

car show
3

games tour 4

farm show
5

parent's day meeting 6

drive-inn 7

media arcade
8

health promo 9

b:k.

sales promo
convention theatre   10

alma-matter school, media bistro bananza party 11

school event
12

* emergency drill.....

dance
13

pic-nic
14

prefered customer card theams to select/ticket

customer line up area with tote rack/seats

modern fryers
should be almost
cordeless. cords
need to be kept in
a wrap or tube that
greece can not
settle on. cordes
must be plugged in
at least 3.5 feet off
the floor with vats
slanted so greese is
draining
automatically into
containers small for
recycling.

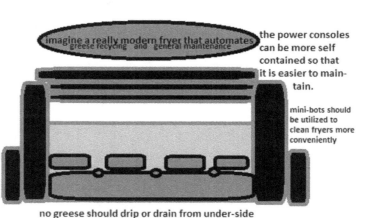

imagine a really modern fryer that automates
greese recycing   and   general maintenance

the power consoles
can be more self
contained so that
it is easier to main-
tain.

mini-bots should
be utilized to
clean fryers more
conveniently

no greese should drip or drain from under-side

musical oven

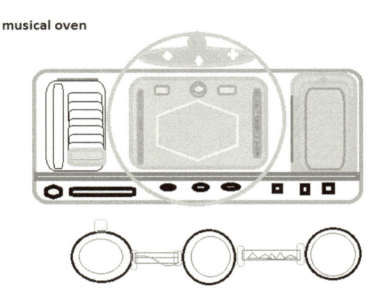

the cafe is semi-automated so that
no one touches the food and all
portions are measured from a
sterilized container

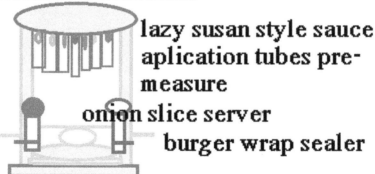

lazy susan style sauce
aplication tubes pre-
measure

onion slice server

burger wrap sealer

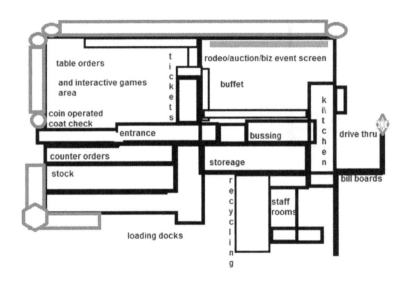

Burger
PALACE

table orders

and interactive games
area

coin operated
coat check

tickets

entrance

counter orders

stock

rodeo/auction/biz event screen

buffet

bussing

storeage

kitchen

drive thru

bill boards

recycling

staff
rooms

loading docks

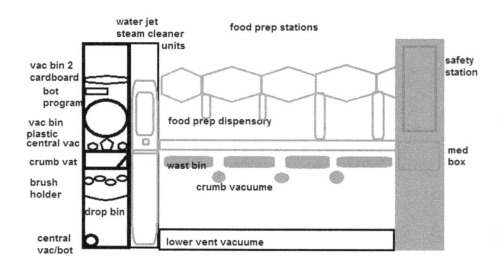

water jet
steam cleaner
units

food prep stations

vac bin 2
cardboard
bot
program

safety
station

vac bin
plastic
central vac

food prep dispensory

crumb vat

med
box

brush
holder

wast bin

crumb vacuume

drop bin

central
vac/bot

lower vent vacuume

all food prep areas etc are cleaned by magnetic robots and
also each prep area ovens etc have cleaning stations right
beside them and fire safety units too

grid to hang any clean ing tools

greese resistant spatter guard

no frys etc may fall behind

orange magnetic cleaning bars

cup dis- pens ory

program and power bar

holding level

fry bin

dip for any cleaning picks and scrapers

salt shakers

tong bar

stock cabinet

protection so no trash or drop waste gathers under unit

drip proof and stucco proof fry bin

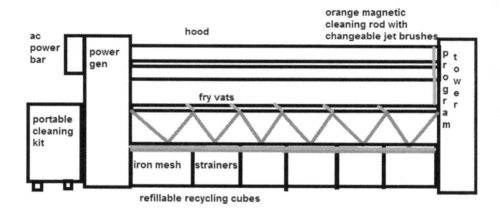

ac
power
bar

hood

orange magnetic
cleaning rod with
changeable jet brushes

power
gen

Program tower

portable
cleaning
kit

fry vats

iron mesh   strainers

refillable recycling cubes

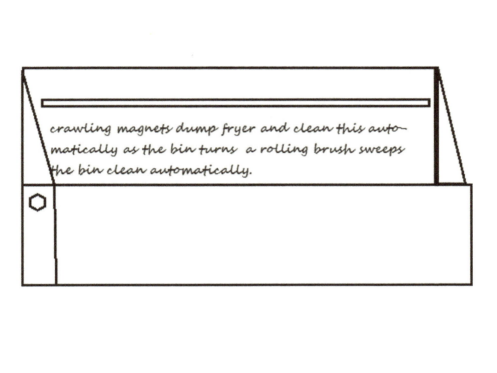

crawling magnets dump fryer and clean this automatically as the bin turns a rolling brush sweeps
the bin clean automatically.

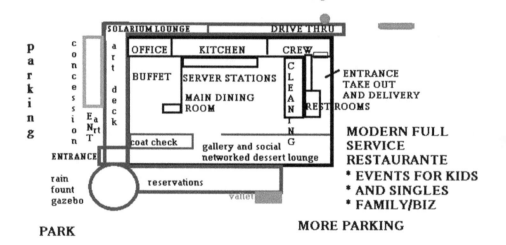

parking

concession

art deck

SOLARIUM LOUNGE

DRIVE THRU

OFFICE | KITCHEN | CREW

BUFFET | SERVER STATIONS

C
L
E
A
N
I
N
G

ENTRANCE
TAKE OUT
AND DELIVERY

MAIN DINING
ROOM

REST ROOMS

ENT

E
a
N rt
T

coat check

gallery and social
networked dessert lounge

MODERN FULL
SERVICE
RESTAURANTE
* EVENTS FOR KIDS
* AND SINGLES
* FAMILY/BIZ

ENTRANCE

rain
fount
gazebo

reservations

valet

PARK

MORE PARKING

Petition

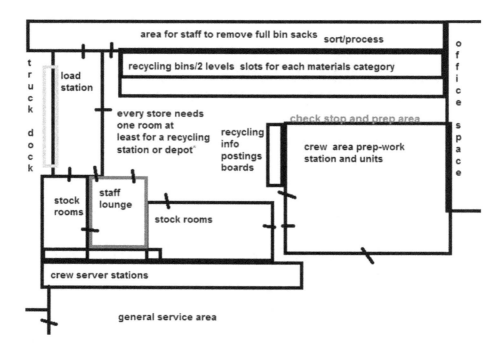

area for staff to remove full bin sacks   sort/process

recycling bins/2 levels slots for each materials category

t
r
u
c
k

d
o
c
k

load
station

every store needs
one room at
least for a recycling
station or depot*

recycling
info
postings
boards

check stop and prep area

crew area prep-work
station and units

o
f
f
i
c
e

s
p
a
c
e

stock
rooms

staff
lounge

stock rooms

crew server stations

general service area

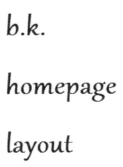

b.k.

homepage

layout

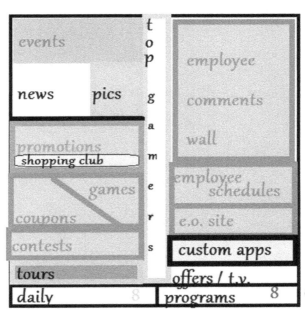

events

news   pics

promotions
shopping club

games

coupons

contests

tours

daily   8

t
o
p

g
a
m
e
r
s

employee

comments

wall

employee
        schedules

e.o. site

custom apps

offers / t.v.

programs   8

Need more programs or features? A different Office suite can
be purchased by clicking the Purchase button above.

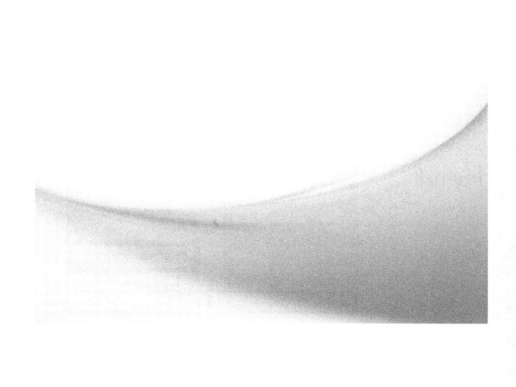

CUSTOMER SERVICE SURVEY

How likely are you to buy, use, or recommend as a gift the following? (1 is least likely, 14 is most likely)

- Personalized preorder and coupon ad cell phone apps
  1 2 3 4 5 6 7 8 9 10 11 12 13 14
- Go Green investors kit
  1 2 3 4 5 6 7 8 9 10 11 12 13 14
- BK biz lunch logo news
  1 2 3 4 5 6 7 8 9 10 11 12 13 14
- More customer service promos with novelty mementos
  1 2 3 4 5 6 7 8 9 10 11 12 13 14
- Social networking site
  1 2 3 4 5 6 7 8 9 10 11 12 13 14
- Customer car wash ticket
  1 2 3 4 5 6 7 8 9 10 11 12 13 14
- A Burger King logo vacation resort
  1 2 3 4 5 6 7 8 9 10 11 12 13 14
- BK novelties or videos from a coin-operated machine
  1 2 3 4 5 6 7 8 9 10 11 12 13 14
- Table service coupons
  1 2 3 4 5 6 7 8 9 10 11 12 13 14
- Preferred-customer card with ad-mail bonus
  1 2 3 4 5 6 7 8 9 10 11 12 13 14
- Custom coupon gift set
  1 2 3 4 5 6 7 8 9 10 11 12 13 14
- Singlet washrooms with an automatic occupied sign
  1 2 3 4 5 6 7 8 9 10 11 12 13 14
- BK singles club apps
  1 2 3 4 5 6 7 8 9 10 11 12 13 14
- Deli delivery or home-party catering or custom home care
  1 2 3 4 5 6 7 8 9 10 11 12 13 14
- Twenty-four-hour service venue with games or midway arcade or other entertainments
  1 2 3 4 5 6 7 8 9 10 11 12 13 14
- BK social media site(s)
  1 2 3 4 5 6 7 8 9 10 11 12 13 14
- BK logo car care kits or travel kit novelties
  1 2 3 4 5 6 7 8 9 10 11 12 13 14
- BK Toyland videos
  1 2 3 4 5 6 7 8 9 10 11 12 13 14
- Valet service window ticket
  1 2 3 4 5 6 7 8 9 10 11 12 13 14
- Auto show trophy club novelty with BK newsletter
  1 2 3 4 5 6 7 8 9 10 11 12 13 14
- A condominium with a BK food court pavilion
  1 2 3 4 5 6 7 8 9 10 11 12 13 14

YORKTON ENVIRONMENT DIRECTORATE
INVITATION TO SUPPORT GO GREEN
CAMPAIGNS GLOBALLY

Please take time to fill out, share, and return a copy of this survey on how customer services packages can be more personalized and economically reasonable.

- Learn how making a purchase can help you earn a profit or investment return.
- Join a social networking website at your favorite dining room and travel stop when camping.
- Take action now. Your social life may appreciate in value.

Do you know how to invest so you can afford extra expenses over the holiday season?

Have you ever considered what a bioethical holistic economic model is?
The foundation of such models is the fundamentalist belief that all life energy is a form of creative art, and not one moment of anyone's time should ever be wasted. Time—every moment of this has real, tangible value. You must use all your creative potential to nourish yourself and serve others. Creative potential units are bricks with a price. You are paid anytime you choose to use those bricks by building customized communications channels on social networking website templates.

Do you believe you can profit by spending time as a consumer?
You can. Every time you use a debit card, you are investing in a customer security or customer care bond. Those invested dollars can fuel the transport services you need to get there, as well as other investment options available to clients who may or may not buy shares options. The company surplus can be reinvested so each customer receives an invested-interests return when they participate in preferred-customer programming, from answering surveys to playing video games. Your customer participation points have value.

Game development society
If you would like to join with others that would like to expand game design education to persons under the poverty line, join this group and subscribe to this

Go Green campaign social networking newsletter.
Investing in a preferred-customer card

This card is your annual credit pass and can be used to make corporate investment decisions, vote, answer polls, pay bills, or enter a gaming or other event. It is also your travel club passport and can be encoded as a sport club or resort door key. Each cardholder can be updated on customer services benefits if you decide to use it as a network pass and decide to send in a customer request as you would like to have the service made available. To show support, sign here:

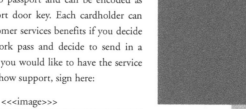

<<<image>>>

DOES YOUR EXPENDITURES CALENDAR REALLY BALANCE SO YOU HAVE A SAVINGS SURPLUS?

newsletter text here.

When you spend money, you do deserve an investment return from your expense account.

Are you looking for more convenient ways to manage your financial goals? Social calendar? Education agenda?

Are you looking for a new investment adventure?

Do modern social networking sites interest you at all?

<<<image>>>

Is this website attractive enough in principle to inspire you to make a commitment to sign up?

Once you have completed your poll, you are also invited to join our social networking group.

It is our objective to effect social change and political change so that our economy is more unified and profitably beneficial in a meaningful way on a daily constitutional basis.

We invite you to participate in more forums and discussions on how each person can help to expand customer services so that customers are considered preferred investors that can turn a profit through the venue's social network.

Type your call-out text here. Consider including customer testimonials or information what you do here.

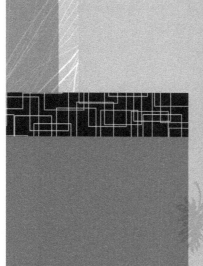

How can you support holistic business initiatives?

Learn to earn. Every moment counts.

When you participate in any survey project, you are making a statement that as a citizen, you have full right and authority to express your reasonable concerns to uphold the law and support administrative systems that complement that directive. You share your information, time, concern, gifted knowledge, your belief in due process. You are supportive as long as you participate in related discourse and as long as you give your permission to share your survey statistics, information in addition, and your comments.

P: 306 890 0435
E: skylark.nf@gmail.com

A: 4119 Broadway St. West
Yorkton, Sask. S3N 0M3

W:
https://sites.google.com/site/yorktonenvironmentdirectorate/

<<<image>>>

Biotecture
innovations
consulting

Petition   July 4, 2011

    I, _____, hereby claim and state that I, as named in the underlined portion of this document, agree to support this petition and any other likewise petition to make it law that in every city, municipality, town, etc., that rents apartments or other venues or dwellings to residents, key holders or a tenants' association must be lawfully established to make certain that rental units are provided to all in need based on a customized request application. Each rental unit must receive ad-mail so all residential services are supplied. By customized regulation, all benefits of citizenship and also income supplement and guild affiliation are accommodated. Also, all tenants must receive a tax credit for rent paid and also an investment return for a portion of rent invested no less than 30 percent of the total rent. And each rental property must have a recycling service or depo that also customizes a service contract for each individual rentor.

Signature: _____
Date: _____
Location: _____
Residence: _____
_____
Contact phone number(s): _____
Fax or alternate contacts (include e-mail): _____
_____
_____
_____

    Please feel free to join this fair-trade symposium and make as many copies of this petition to share with others as you would like. The petition, when you are done, may be mailed signed to your local MLA or member of parliament. You may also send the petition to the prime minister of Canada or speaker of the house or Senate Canada or Saskatchewan Cultural Industries Development Council, 114-2001 Cornwall Street, Regina, Saskatchewan S4P 3X9.

House of Commons
Speaker of the House
Ottawa Ontario
K1A 0A2

Compliments of
Yorkton Environment Directorate
4 119 Broadway St. West
Yorkton, SK, S3N 0M3
1-306-890-0435

Petition courtesy of Yorkton Environment Directorate.

Speaker of the house, please consider my signature on this page, notice of my agreement with this petition, and any other likewise petition that it become federal law, respected in each province to provide a tax credit to all persons that have to rent their primary place of residence. I agree also that a portion of rent should be invested through a tenants' association that guarantees ad-mail packages guarantee all tenants rights to all benefits of citizenship so each tenant and landlord has a dividend return.

Name	Address and e-mail/fax	Phone

Please make copies and return signed:
Yorkton Environment Directorate, 4 119 Broadway St. W S3N 0M3 1-306-890-0435

July 10, 2011

Greetings, federation director,

    I am hoping that all your bands can help distribute this petition on their tours. But if even only one member could take this mission on, as a citizen, that would make me happy. Please share the petition with your office staff and associates as I would like your assistance so that distribution of this petition can be increased. Thank you for your kind attention to this matter. We all should support this new petition to guarantee that no one is economically disadvantaged or discriminated against in Canada. If you would like to take the issue to world government supporters and international law associations, that also would be helpful. Have a blessed day. Keep the torch of peace burning in all your gateways and at all your fountains.

Yorkton Environment Directorate
4119 Broadway St. West
Yorkton, Saskatchewan
S3N 0M3

Petition   July 6, 2011

    I, _____, residing at _____
in the city of _____
declare I do lawfully support this general petition to make it a statute of
this country that every city license maintains a social club for single persons
of all income levels that will provide educational support, professional
networking services, and professional social networking services to all
single persons equally, without bias toward income level.

    I agree all single persons have the right to free assembly to find a
suitable spouse to pursue a lawful and sustainable means of an income
together. All single persons need a social networking forum to assist them
in finding a suitable partner for professional gain and maintenance of
personal well-being. Professional development seminars for singles should
be hosted at least once per month, free of charge, at a venue where alcohol
is not served. Persons aged sixteen and above may attend without parental
consent.

<<<image>>>
This petition has been drafted at
Yorkton Environment Directorate
4119 Broadway St. West, Yorkton, Saskatchewan
S3N 0M3 1-306-890-0435
Please make as many copies of this petition as you can and forward a
signature list to the above address. Thank you.
Noelle Finnerty
633-737-143

Professional photography landscape design, and holistic biotectuture Consulting

Skylark.nf@gmail.com

CONSULTING WITH RESULTS.

"Would you enjoy spending time in a guarden or solarium with as many locally grown products as you desired? Would you like a music video made to display your guarden Would you enjoy gardening indoors through the winter? Do you need a place in your yard cultivated so you may safely maintain livestock or pets? Call us we can help you with service and supplies"

Here you may meet persons that will help you design guarden space to meet any personal, professional, wholeistic or seasonal need that you have. Consultants are certified through DETC programming center.

We have a wide range of networked professionals ready to work with you so you may harvest the best results from custom designed ornamental or botanical gardens you would like to add to your property in any outdoor or indoor location.

We can also assist you with indoor/outdoor art installation projects. Permanent or temporary.

For personal, home sales party & other occasions

4 119 BROADWAY ST WEST • Yorkton, Sask S3N 0M3 • 306 890 0435
•http://amazingwebwarehousecom.biz

We need musicians and drivers to work with our catering group. If you are available to work on call, contact Noelle at 1-306-890-0435.

Think about this: what is your dream for?

Yourself? Your family? Your community? Your country? Your world?

Greetings, readers,

This is a book about how every city should make certain that most of its restaurant venues have specific services for all citizens in the area. It states that all venues should be socialized so that all needs of the client are met on an individual basis. Policy includes even credit investment counseling so that every dollar spent is an investment, not just a payment for service rendered by an hourly rate. It is a proposal to encourage all business owners to develop holistic, innovative, interactive, and mutually profitable management policy. This type of venue should have been licensed since 1975 to prevent erosion from any economic recession preset. It is a truly innovative and inspired proposal for all citizens to consider.

I have been hosting discussions on how business venues need to encourage economic reforms and the development of holistic media services to specific membership groups or warehouse clubs since 1970. I enjoy co-op art poetry and writing reviews on educational program reforms in my spare time. I encourage more land use development groups to support the development of warehouse clubs with a twenty-four-hour operations policy.

<<<image>>>
Noelle Finnerty
4119 Broadway St. West
Yorkton, Sask. S3N 0M3
Social development critic